Flesh and Stone

GENERAL EDITOR
DEBORAH DEFORD

BOOK DESIGNER
BARBARA MARKS

STONY CREEK GRANITE QUARRY WORKERS CELEBRATION

STONY CREEK, CONNECTICUT

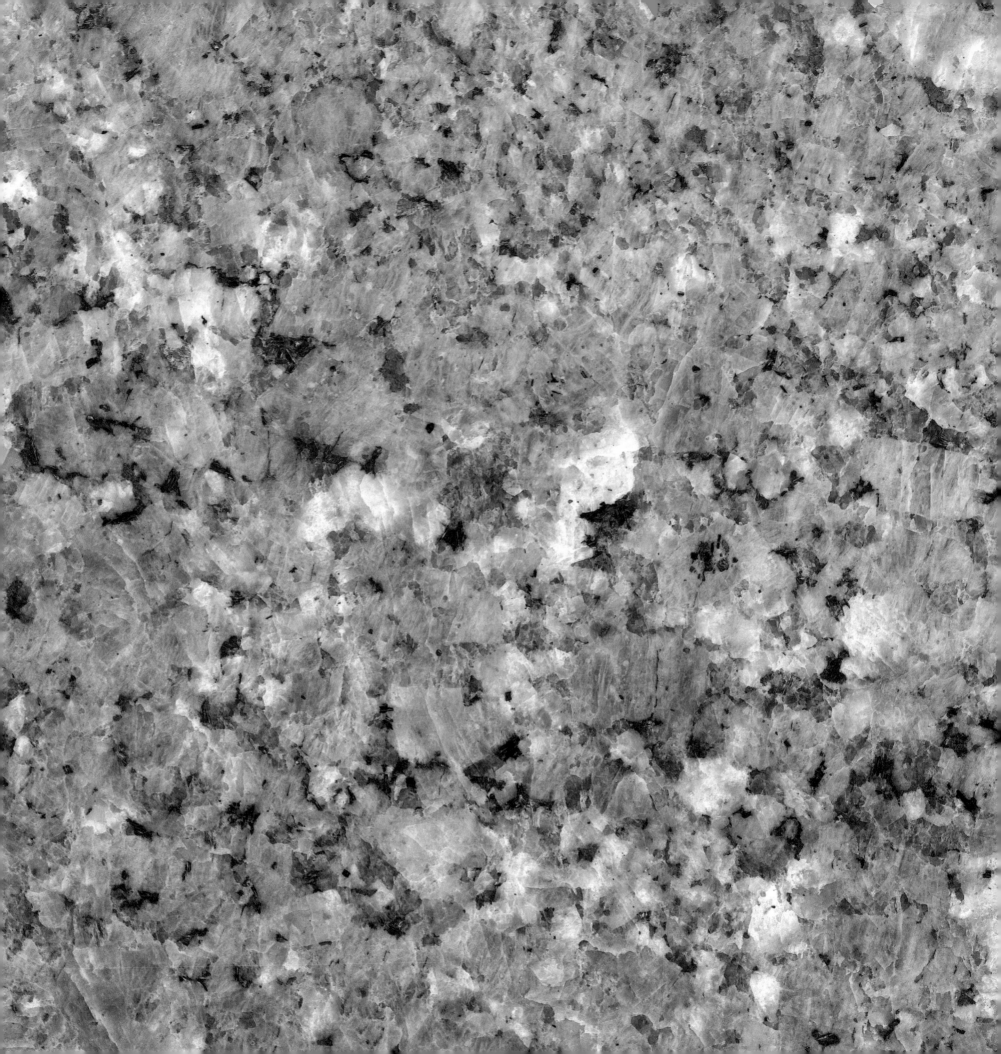

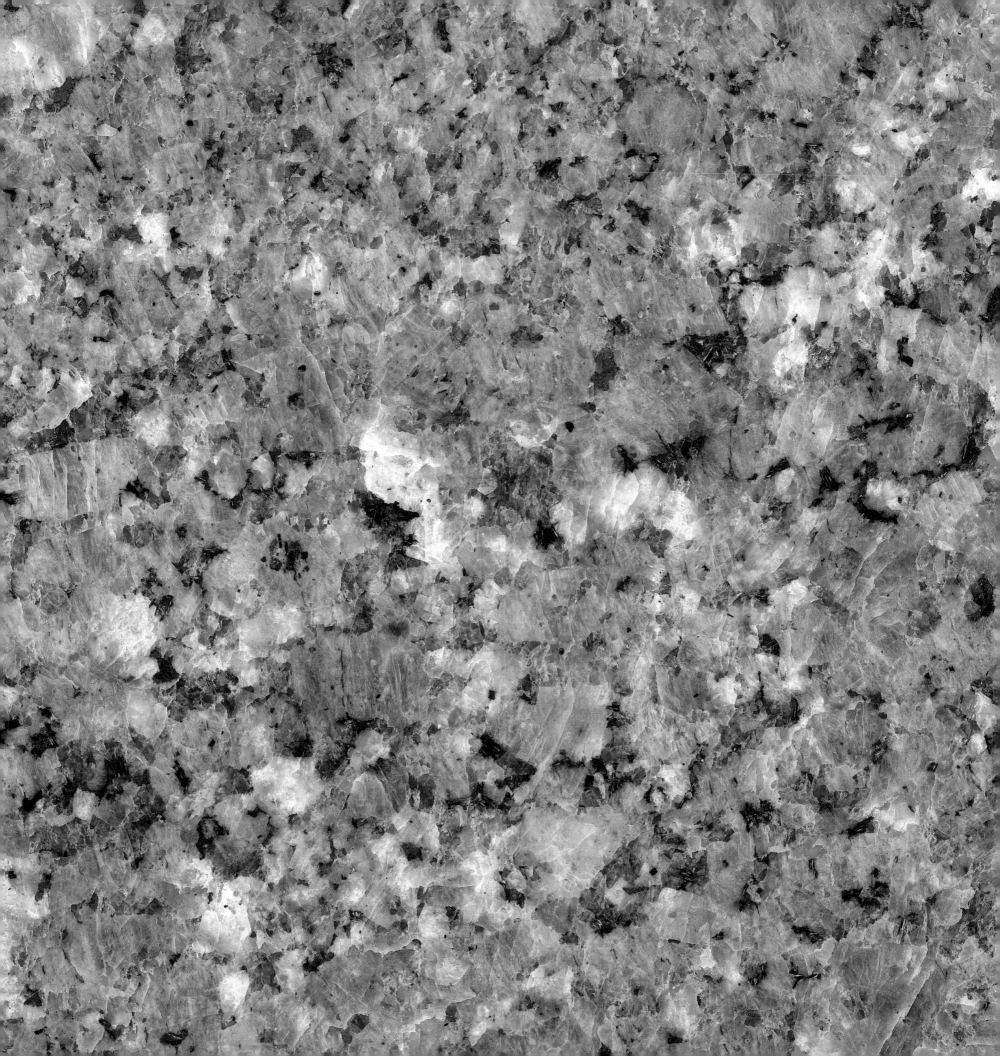

Flesh and Stone

STONY CREEK

AND THE AGE OF GRANITE

Flesh and Stone: Stony Creek and the Age of Granite

BOOK DESIGN BY BARBARA MARKS

EDITED BY DEBORAH DEFORD

Published by
Stony Creek Granite Quarry Workers Celebration,
Box 3047, Stony Creek, CT 06405 in association with
Leete's Island Books, Box 3131, Stony Creek, CT 06405

www.quarrycelebration.org
www.leetesisland.com

LIBRARY OF CONGRESS CARD NUMBER: 00-110390

ISBN: 0-918172-29-2

PRINTED IN ITALY BY AMILCARE PIZZI, S.P.A., MILANO

To the people of the quarries—
the owners, laborers, families, and friends
who braved the granite to build a legacy

CONTENTS

Look to the rock you were hewn from,
To the quarry you were dug from.

ISAIAH 51:1

HOW THIS BOOK CAME TO BE

CONNECTICUT

Stony Creek

Across several miles of Connecticut shoreline and extending into Long Island Sound stretches a formation of pink granite that one hundred and fifty years ago propelled a region into the industrial revolution. The granite, known as "Stony Creek pink," brought hundreds and more immigrants to the area and precipitated the opening of numerous private and commercial granite quarries, one of which continues to operate up to the present. In the process, it changed the face of an entire region and sent its products around the world.

This is the story of a transformation that was repeated in myriad ways across the United States beginning in the middle of the nineteenth century. It is also the story of community and change as it was experienced in one small region centered in the Branford, Stony Creek, and Guilford areas of Connecticut. And it is the story of the modern community of Stony Creek and the decision of some of its citizens to remember local history in a meaningful and lasting way.

As the turn of the millennium approached, a number of "Creekers" put their heads together to consider how they might honor their village, its environs, and the past both embody. The planning group found themselves especially captivated by the legacy of the quarries, and the extent to which the impact of the industry continues to be felt even now. As they dug deeper, they discovered a rich lode of primary sources, including individuals who actually worked in the old quarries and first generation descendants of quarry workers. Queries yielded a great body of anecdotal material about the quarries' heyday, vintage photographs, antique tools, artifacts, and hardware, quarry and town records, and architectural legacies. The planners settled on the "Stony Creek Granite Quarry Workers Celebration" as their theme, then put together a dedicated team of volunteers to accomplish their aim of a lasting memorial to the local past.

The project, as it turned out, has had as rich and varied an output as the history it remembers. The community has pulled together enthusiastic support for an aggregate of events and products that collectively bear certification as an official White House Millennium Project of local history—the first awarded in the state of Connecticut. Thanks to the generosity of both individuals and granting organizations (see page 190), the financial challenges have all been met.

The Stony Creek Granite Quarry Workers Celebration launched its efforts with an exhibit of more than 100 vintage images and numerous quarry-related artifacts at the Willoughby Wallace Memorial Library in Stony Creek.

A local educator contributed hands-on components to the exhibit specially designed for the participation of school children. Over the course of a month, hundreds of individuals, families, and children visited the exhibit. As a culmination to the show, the framed and matted images (all reproduced from original antique photographs) were dispersed by silent auction, an event that brought a standing-room only crowd for the closing day of the exhibit and an enlivened interest in the area's nineteenth-century history. In the process, the exhibit whetted appetites for a lasting, accessible collection of the images that had been displayed. A book about the quarry era made such a collection possible.

Meanwhile, the planning committee organized a series of "conversaziones" on various aspects of the quarry history—economic and social issues, the work of quarrying, local life in the quarries' heyday, immigration, geological background, and architectural output. The series kicked off during the exhibit's run and continued for a year, including several "field trips" to sites where Stony Creek pink granite has been put to architectural use, filling the seats for every talk, and bringing ongoing energy to the overall effort. These speakers would later become the roster of authors telling the story in published form.

At the same time, the planning committee commissioned a series of interviews to be conducted of surviving quarry workers and their descendants. These conversations were video- and audio-recorded, then transcribed, with the intent of capturing the personal experiences and memories of aging eyewitnesses. The accounts have provided valuable information and moving illustrations of a time of great restlessness, productivity, and change. Donated to local historical archives, the histories also bring life and color to the unfolding tale the quarry era, and many are excerpted in the pages to follow.

Perhaps most lasting of the "Celebration's" output are an architectural monument and the book before you. The former will keep in sight of the community a tribute to a time and the hard-working people who lived through it. Its inspiration came from a number of notably lovely architectural elements of pink granite that had been discarded on the outskirts of one of the local quarries and only recently rediscovered. A subcommittee of Stony Creek artists, designers, and architects submitted an innovative plan to create an outdoor sculptural monument at the Willoughby Wallace Library that functions both as art and exterior furnishings.

The book, *Flesh and Stone: Stony Creek and the Age of Granite,* looks not only at the life and times of the regions' quarries, but considers an entire era, with all its drama and charm. The contributing team of writers includes a Yale geologist, a Harvard historian, a local historian/minister, a medical doctor, an expert on the human factors of work, a descendant of quarry workers, the Guilford town historian, and an architectural historian. Produced by a professional writer/editor and a professional book designer—both inhabitants of Stony Creek who, like the authors, donated their time and effort—the book brings together a picture in microcosm of a surge of people, politics, and productivity that took the nation by storm.

The Stony Creek Granite Quarry Workers Celebration in all its aspects has been a vehicle of remembrance for this small community, and it has become a further building block of the very community it celebrates. It is local history captured and local history in the making, a living monument to time and place and the people who enliven both. On behalf of all those who planned and contributed to the effort, I invite you here to enter another time and meet a remarkable group of people who, as individuals and in concert, helped shape the world in which you live.

—DEBORAH DEFORD, *General Editor*

December 2000

A NOTE TO OUR READERS:

Recorded history, like the lives and events it chronicles, is an evolving story. New discoveries and new interpretations of existing records inevitably add information, accuracy, and insight over time to the story of the past as we know it. In *Flesh and Stone: Stony Creek and the Age of Granite,* both producers and contributors have made every effort to ensure the accuracy and authenticity of the material presented here. Many hours went into primary research and fact-checking to make this possible. We acknowledge, however, that this history—like all history—will reflect the foibles and embellishments of both written records and human memory. For all the hard work devoted to truth-telling, we offer our thanks. For any mistakes that remain, we apologize and look to future investigators who can set the record straight.

CONTRIBUTORS

This book developed as a collaboration in every regard, including its authorship. The contributing authors brought not only their talents and expertise to the enterprise of research and writing, but their distinctive styles, as well.

To maintain the richness of the multivoiced narrative, we have arranged the text as an ongoing conversation among enthusiasts. A signature monogram identifies the speaker at the end of each portion of the story; the key below identifies these dedicated contributors:

JA *Jay Ague, PhD,* Associate Professor, Department of Geology and Geophysics, and Curator of Mineralogy, Peabody Museum of Natural History, Yale University

AD *Anthony "Unk" DaRos,* First Selectman, Town of Branford, descendant of Stony Creek quarry workers and former quarry worker

RD *Ronald DeFord, PhD,* Internal Consultant, human factors of work, Northeast Utilities

PDH *Peter Dobkin Hall, PhD,* Hauser Lecturer in Public Policy at the John F. Kennedy School of Government, Harvard University

JEH *Joel E. Helander,* Municipal Historian for the Town of Guilford, and a twelfth-generation descendant of several of the town's founding families

JH *John Herzan, AM,* Architectural Historian and National Register Coordinator, Connecticut Historical Commission

WJ *Wayne Jacobson, MDiv,* Pastor of the Church of Christ Congregational, Stony Creek, Connecticut

JBK *John B. Kirby Jr.* author of works in the fields of art, architecture, and history, including numerous publications about the history of Stony Creek

MZ *Marvin Zimmerman, MD,* medical doctor and local historian, Branford, Connecticut

THE PRODUCERS

Deborah DeFord, a recipient of the American Antiquarian Society Fellowship for Historical Research by Creative and Performing Artists and Writers, has worked in publishing as an author and editor for more than 20 years.

Barbara Marks has been designing and producing books from her studio in Stony Creek for 22 years.

INTRODUCTION

This celebration of photographs, anecdotes, and reflections is the collaborative effort of a community that wants to capture and preserve the memories and experiences of a time gone by. It is a piece of Americana that portrays the shaping of a nation. It is about an industry that encompassed all the trades and involved people of every economic and social background.

The stone quarries of Guilford, Branford, and Stony Creek could be described as the melting pot to which our history books so often refer, where nationalities and cultures came together.

The common goal of these industrious folks was to provide for themselves and their families. They met this goal by extracting from the earth the hard, unrelenting, and unforgiving mineral known as granite—a mineral that was formed by fire in the bowels of the planet.

These newcomers invaded the quiet farming and fishing villages with the machines and technology of the young industrial revolution. New businesses and services sprang up, along with an immediate housing shortage. Boardinghouses became the norm, introducing a new culture. Of all the villages, Stony Creek felt the greatest impact, with lasting effects.

Any granite outcropping has the potential to produce a reasonable product. Each of the region's locations has its own characteristics—whether in color, coarseness, or hardness—and it appears that the stoneworkers exploited most granite sites to some degree or another.

Over time, the demand for stone fell off because of changing costs of steel and labor and the advent of concrete building construction. Many quarrymen, while staying in the area, took jobs in other trades or in manufacturing plants such as the iron factory or the wire mill in Branford. A few New England quarries, including one located in Stony Creek, continue to operate and employ quarry workers, although at a greatly reduced level.

This book is dedicated to that hardy breed known as quarrymen. Their labors scarred the local landscape but produced the most elegant edifices that remain standing today—these will continue for many generations to come.

—ANTHONY "UNK" DAROS
First Selectman, Town of Branford

Flesh and Stone

Summer has nearly deserted Stony Creek.

But on a late day of warmth that inspires fall housecleaning, tempts the children to play hooky, and raises a sweat on the laborers' brows, the clear air is suddenly torn by the shriek of a steam whistle. Something has happened at the quarry. The schoolteacher loses her place in the book she is reading aloud to her students. A shopkeeper exchanges a wary glance with his customer. A nursing mother's head snaps up. And she utters a prayer that is repeated by a hundred other quarry wives: "Please, God, don't let it be bad. Don't let it be *him*."

IN THE BEGINNING

FLESH AGAINST STONE

At some point in time, long before people started keeping written records, someone wanted a chunk of stone. Most likely looking for material to build himself shelter, he decided that instead of gathering a rock that had already been broken free from a ledge by water, weather, ice, or tree root, he would harvest a piece from the earth itself.

Perhaps it was laziness. Breaking off a piece of nearby ledge may have been more appealing to him than lugging freestanding rock from a distance. Or perhaps he needed a certain size and shape of rock, and he believed in his ability to extract the perfect specimen from a jutting ledge.

Whatever the reason, at some point in time, flesh and bone decided to cleave stone from the earth.

At first, it was a matter of brute force—especially if the harvester was not too particular. Pounding with a rock against a stony jut would either free more stone or drive the worker to another outcropping. Eventually, by trying different juts, people learned that certain kinds of rock were easier than others to free. They also found that most stone had rift (horizontal proclivity) and grain (vertical proclivity).

For centuries, people settled for the softer and grainier stones. Over time, they learned how to put wood into crevices, add water, and let the swelling wood split harder stone—imitating tree roots and frost wedging. When they lost patience with slow-swelling wood, they learned how to drive stone or wooden wedges into the cracks. And when they developed the skills to make metals, they created superior wedges.

By the time people began to quarry granite in the Stony Creek area, their ancestors had already built pyramids, temples, roads, and cathedrals. Yet little had changed in the technology used to extract stone from the ground. Even so, these latest of the harvesters dared to take on one of the most stubborn of stones. They put iron and steel between their flesh and the stone and bit into the hard face of the Earth. Before long, they would adopt newer methods that could harvest the stone at unprecedented levels and, in so doing, make it possible to meet the demands of a growing nation.

—RD

Fred Fasset swinging a sledge hammer while Louis Balestracci holds a bullset

7

EARTH FORCES

The story of Stony Creek granite begins hundreds of millions of years ago, when what we know as Africa, South America, Australia, India, the southeastern United States, and parts of China and Europe were linked. Together they formed an enormous continental mass called "Gondwana" or "Gondwanaland," named for a zone of specific rocks in India.

Geology, the science of the Earth, allows us to trace the origins of Stony Creek granite back through a complex sequence of geologic events that spanned some 600 million years of Earth history. Preserved within the rocks is a detailed record of volcanic upheavals, earthquakes, mountain building, and continental drift that can be read using modern methods of geologic research. To understand Stony Creek granite, we need to consider how the granite formed, what it is made of, and how it ended up in New England on the eastern fringe of North America. The great beauty and strength that distinguish Stony Creek granite resulted from a unique progression of dynamic Earth processes that operated at intense pressures and temperatures deep within ancient mountain belts.

THE GRANITE FORMS

During mountain building, parts of the deep Earth become so hot and chemically reactive that rocks can partially melt. The molten rock, called *magma,* is less dense than its surroundings, and so it rises toward the Earth's surface (much as air bubbles rise through water), sometimes as quickly as 10 feet (about 3 m) per year. Some magmas ascend all the way to the surface of the Earth. These become *lava* as they erupt out on to the land, forming volcanos. Other magmas cool off and solidify (crystallize) slowly underground before they reach the surface, forming large masses of rock called *plutons*—named for Pluto, the Greek god of the underworld. Rocks that form by the cooling and solidification of magma or lava are called *igneous rocks.*

Stony Creek granite is just such a pluton that solidified before it reached the Earth's surface. The melting that produced the granite magma probably occurred at temperatures of at least 1,300 degrees Fahrenheit (about 700°C) deep within the Earth. Geologic evidence suggests that the melting and magma ascent occurred some

600 million years ago. This makes Stony Creek granite one of the oldest rocks exposed anywhere in New England, despite its relative youth compared to the total age of the Earth—about 4.55 billion years. When this granite formed, only the most primitive animals existed, inhabiting ancient oceans. The granite magma solidified under at least 10 to 15 miles (16 to 24 km) of rock at pressures thousands of times greater than that of the atmosphere around us. Countless centuries of erosion by wind, water, and glaciers stripped off the overlying rock to expose the deeply formed granite at the surface where we see it today.

A SUITE OF MINERALS

Rocks are simply aggregates of one or more kinds of minerals. Granites are igneous rocks composed of relatively large crystals of a specific suite of minerals. To better understand what this means, it is important to define the terminology.

Crystals are among the most beautiful and fascinating phenomena of the natural world. When the ancient Greeks found crystals of quartz high in the mountains where it was cold all year long, they reasoned that these crystals were ice that the extreme cold had permanently frozen. Although our word *crystal* can be traced back to the Greek word *krystallos,* meaning

"ice," we know a great deal more about crystals than the ancients did. Crystals have been the subject of intense study because of their intrinsic beauty, economic value, and importance to industry. Basically, a crystal is a solid, bounded by flat (planar) faces, and composed of a regular, highly ordered, three-dimensional arrangement of atoms. The great internal order of a crystal's atomic structure creates its striking symmetrical appearance.

The definition of a *mineral* closely relates to that of a crystal. A mineral is a naturally formed, nonliving solid that has a characteristic chemical composition and crystal structure. All minerals occur as crystals, but not all crystals are minerals. For example, sugar crystals that grow to make "rock candy" are *not* minerals—they are made by humans and therefore not "naturally formed."

In granite, the process of "crystallization" occurs as the granite magma cools and freezes solid. Eventually, no molten rock remains, leaving the magma completely solidified. Imagine liquid water as "molten ice," analogous to the liquid "molten rock" of a granite magma. When water cools below its freezing point, ice crystals grow from the liquid until no liquid is left. Only solid ice remains. Of course, the freezing temperature of a granite magma—around 1,150 degrees Fahrenheit (about 620°C)—far

9

exceeds that for water. A key characteristic of granite is that it contains mineral crystals large enough to be easily visible to the unaided eye. The crystals are large because they had a long time to grow while the granite magma slowly cooled below the Earth's surface.

All granites contain roughly equal proportions of three common minerals. The reddish mineral so exquisitely developed in Stony Creek granite is called *potassium feldspar,* made mostly of potassium, silicon, aluminum, and oxygen. Its reddish color comes from traces of iron in the structure of the mineral. The cream-colored or light gray mineral is called *plagioclase feldspar,* and its primary constituents are sodium, calcium, silicon, aluminum, and oxygen. *Quartz*—the third major mineral—is the medium to dark gray, translucent mineral in the granite, composed almost entirely of silicon and oxygen. All three minerals are very hard and, when fresh and unweathered, unscratchable by even a good steel knife blade. This extraordinary hardness accounts for the durability of the granite. But the size and color of the three minerals can vary widely from one granite to the next. As a result, some granites,

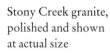

Stony Creek granite, polished and shown at actual size

such as Stony Creek granite, achieve greater beauty than others, even though all granites share similar minerals and chemical composition.

Granites may also contain at least one or more dark-colored minerals. Stony Creek granite contains *biotite,* a dark brown to black mineral rich in potassium, iron, magnesium, silicon, aluminum, and oxygen. The dark color results from large amounts of iron and magnesium in the atomic structure of the mineral. In addition, the granite may contain minor amounts of dark, oxygen-rich minerals with a metallic appearance that are also rich in iron, and sometimes titanium. One of these, called *magnetite* (or lodestone), has magnetic properties and will actually attract a small magnet suspended on a string. The dark biotite and magnetite crystals interspersed among the relatively light-colored quartz and feldspars provide the striking visual contrast so characteristic of Stony Creek granite.

THE MIGRATION OF GRANITE

The Earth's continents move in a constant slow motion—called *continental drift*—across the planet's surface, and have been moving thus for billions of years. Today the outermost shell of the Earth is divided into six major and numerous smaller "plates" of rock, sometimes called *lithospheric plates.* The plates, about 120 miles (about 200 km) thick in continental regions and about 60 miles (about 100 km) thick below ocean basins, move in response to complex forces acting deep within the Earth and arising from our planet's release of heat. Stony Creek granite is now part of the North American plate, an immense mass of rock that includes the United States, Canada, Greenland, eastern Russia, and parts of the Atlantic and Pacific Oceans. However, the granite did not form in its present location, but traveled to New England by continental drift.

The Earth's plates move slowly, but at rates easily measured using today's global positioning satellite (GPS) technology. Speeds range from around one-half to five inches (about 1 to 13 cm) per year. This may not seem like a lot, but over millions of years of geologic time, the distances add up. For example, if a plate moves at 1 inch (2.54 cm) per year for 350 million years, it will travel about 5,500 miles (about 8,850 km)—the distance between Los Angeles and Tokyo. The moving plates interact with one another at their edges—a process described by the theory called *plate tectonics*—and give rise to most of the known earthquake and mountain building processes.

Lithospheric plates may "bump into" other plates. If continents approach one another and eventually collide, the collision can produce high mountains. Today, for example, India is colliding with Asia, forcing up the Himalayan mountain chain. Some scientists argue that the Appalachians—formed by collisions between plates hundreds of millions of years ago—were once as high and rugged as the Himalayas.

In contrast to colliding, a continental land mass may split apart along a great zone of faulting—what geologists call a *rift zone*. Today the Arabian peninsula is splitting away from the African continental land mass along a rift zone that occupies the Red Sea. As a result, Saudi Arabia is moving away from Sudan. Rifting thins the continental crustal rock, causing its height above sea level within the rift zone to drop over time. Eventually, rifts become deep valleys with elevations so low that seawater can enter. Over a long enough period of time—tens of millions of years—rifting can form whole new ocean basins. In Africa, the opening between the rifting continental masses is being filled in by sediments shed from the rocks that surround the rift, by lavas, and by seawater. Scientists cannot predict whether the rifting and spreading will continue long enough to create a large new ocean.

Another kind of boundary between plates forms when oceanic lithosphere collides with continental lithosphere. Because the oceanic rock mass is very dense, it sinks or is thrust under the continent, forming what geologists call a *subduction zone.* As the oceanic rock descends deep within the Earth, it is heated and compressed, causing many complex chemical reactions. At very great temperatures and depths within the Earth, around 100 miles (about 160 km) deep, these reactions can cause rock to melt, forming magmas that ascend and either cool as plutons or erupt as volcanic lavas above the subduction zone. The volcanic mountains of the Andes in South America, for example, are forming where oceanic rock of the Nazca plate is being subducted under the South American plate. The Sierra Nevada range of California formed above an ancient subduction zone, for the most part between 85 million and 110 million years ago.

Great earthquakes can be generated when plates scrape past one another along a "strike-slip" fault line, forming what is known as a *transform boundary.* The San Andreas fault of California, a prime example, formed where the North American plate and the Pacific plate meet. As part of the Pacific plate, Los Angeles is moving northward along the fault relative to the rest of North America. In about 11 million years, Los Angeles will be next to San Francisco.

As it turns out, the geologic development of the Stony Creek area included all of these kinds of plate boundaries—collision zone, rift zone, subduction zone, and transform boundary. Thus Stony Creek granite has one of the most complex histories known for rocks of New England.

The precise origins of Stony Creek granite are surrounded in mystery, but modern geologic studies are providing critical new information. It is now thought that Stony Creek granite and related rocks originated on the edge of Gondwanaland during melting, magma formation, and volcanic activity in a subduction zone setting around 600 million years ago. Surprisingly, the place in which the granite formed was near what is now the northwestern edge of South America. Scientists disagree as to the exact position of North America at this

The continents' positions—according to scientists' approximations—around the time that Stony Creek granite formed, about 600 million years ago

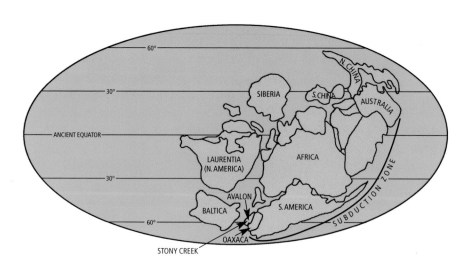

12

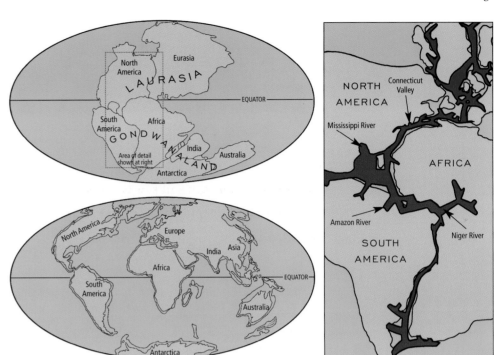

time. Some argue that it was attached to what is now the southeastern part of South America, while others say that it was attached to Africa or Siberia.

Regardless of North America's precise location 600 million years ago, the Stony Creek granite and its surrounding rocks clearly originated far from their present location in Branford. They must have been sliced off the South American continent and then somehow attached to North America. Geologists believe that around 550 million to 600 million years ago, considerable strike-slip motion occurred on the edge of South America. This led to great earthquakes and the separation of the Stony Creek granite and its surroundings from the South American mainland. Through time, this newly separated piece of continent and North America moved closer and closer together. Eventually, they collided with one another, forming a high mountain range that fused the Stony Creek area to eastern North America. This linkage was complete by about 200 million to 300 million years ago. Throughout this complex geologic history, the other continents also moved across the Earth's surface and collided with each other. In fact, by 200 million years ago, northwestern Africa had also collided with eastern North America, wedging the

rocks of the Stony Creek area in a kind of "geologic sandwich."

The geography of the world 200 million years ago was totally unlike that of today. All the continents were joined into a giant "supercontinent" called *Pangea* (pronounced "Panjeeyah"), which is Greek for "all lands." The northern half of Pangea, called *Laurasia* (combining an old term for rocks in Canada's heartland and "Asia"), included most of Europe, Asia, and North America. The southern half of Pangea included most of Gondwanaland. The two halves of Pangea met near the ancient equator, with northwestern Africa connected to eastern North America, and northern South America connected to Mexico and Central America.

The supercontinent Pangea had a relatively brief lifetime, geologically speaking. It became unstable, breaking up into the continental

THE BREAKUP OF PANGEA
Upper left: The giant supercontinent, Pangea, approximately 200 million years ago. *Right:* Close-up of central Pangea, showing the rift zones where the supercontinent split apart. The major rift that separated Africa from the Americas opened to form the Atlantic Ocean. *Lower left:* The continents today.

13

Geology terms to know

collision zone	the location at which one lithospheric plate collides with another	magma	molten rock
continental drift	the movement of continents across the surface of the Earth	mineral	a naturally formed, nonliving solid that has a characteristic chemical composition and crystal structure
crystal	a solid, bounded by flat (planar) faces, composed of a regular, highly ordered, three-dimensional arrangement of atoms	plagioclase feldspar	one of the three minerals found in granite; made mostly of sodium, calcium, silicon, aluminum, and oxygen
Gondwana or Gondwanaland	an enormous, ancient continental mass composed of what we now know as Africa, South America, Australia, India, the southeastern United States, and parts of China and Europe, and named for a zone of specific rocks in India	plate tectonics	the theory that describes how lithospheric plates move
		plutons	masses of rock formed by magma that crystallizes underground
		potassium feldspar	one of the three minerals found in granite; made mostly of potassium, silicon, aluminum, and oxygen
granite	igneous rock that crystallizes underground and is composed of relatively large crystals of a specific suite of minerals	quartz	one of the three minerals found in granite; made mostly of silicon and oxygen
igneous rock	rock formed by the cooling and solidification of magma or lava	rift zone	a zone of tension that acts to pull continental land masses or ocean basins apart
lava	magma that erupts on the Earth's surface; the vent from which the lava emerges is called a volcano	subduction zone	the location at which lithospheric plates sink or are thrust into the Earth's interior
lithospheric plates	plates of rock that form the outermost shell of the Earth; today six major and numerous smaller plates form this shell	transform boundary	the location at which plates scrape past one another along a strike-slip fault line

landmasses we know today. Between about 120 million and 200 million years ago, Africa split away from North America along a giant rift zone, leaving the Stony Creek granite behind, firmly attached to the eastern United States seaboard. Seawater entered the rift, and as the rift slowly widened, the Atlantic Ocean was born. Later, between about 60 million and 120 million years ago, the great geologic rift between North America and Africa spread southward, splitting eastern South America from western Africa and opening up the southern half of the Atlantic Ocean. The Atlantic continues to widen today. The distance between eastern North America and northwestern Africa increases by about an inch (2.54 cm) a year.

The rifting apart of the continents was imperfect—some cracks formed and opened partway but then stopped. One of these "failed rifts" occupies the Connecticut Valley today. This large valley, as much as 20 miles (30 to 35 km) wide and extending from Long Island Sound up through New England, opened and filled up with igneous rocks and sediments as Africa split away. For a while, the elevation of the valley was so low that it was flooded with water. While Africa separated from North America, Earth forces sought to tear southern New England in half, forming many of the famous

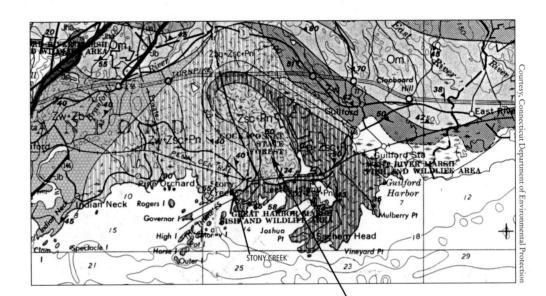

GEOLOGIC MAP OF THE STONY CREEK AREA
The kidney-bean-shaped region is dominated by granite, but much granite can also be found among other kinds of rocks in the surrounding colored areas.

geographical landmarks of Connecticut. The remnants of this geologic activity remain visible along Connecticut's Interstate 91. In the New Haven area, East Rock, West Rock, and the Sleeping Giant are igneous rocks that filled in cracks in the North American continent as it was being torn. Dinosaurs, alive and well at the time, left their footprints in sediments now preserved at Dinosaur State Park.

The long geologic odyssey of Stony Creek granite from South America to New England involved thousands of miles of continental drift across the face of the Earth, and took hundreds of millions of years. At the same time that fresh blocks of massive Stony Creek granite cut from the quarry walls provide building stone of unparalleled quality, they afford us an invaluable record of the ongoing processes that move continents, make mountains, and shape the Earth.

—JA

15

THE BIRTH OF AN INDUSTRY

THE MOST BOUNTEOUS HARVEST

In places like Stony Creek, the soils left behind by the glaciers—heavy with rock and clay—made farming a chancy proposition from the time of earliest settlement. "Saltwater farmers" eked out a bare subsistence by combining small-scale farming, growing orchards, woodcutting, fishing, and such crafts as shoe- and basketmaking, often under contract to local merchants. Occasionally, great events like the American Revolution and the embargo preceding the War of 1812 would offer these poor villagers moments of prosperity—usually based on smuggling and trading with the enemy. But the more common experience for most coastal villagers before the Civil War was of continuous, backbreaking labor that yielded enough to survive but far less than a living.

Yale President Timothy Dwight captured the depressed character of Branford after passing through the town on his way to Cape Cod in 1800. After remarking on the "immense multitudes" of herring caught in Branford water during the months of June and July and praising the fish (in its rotted form) as "the most prolific manure," he described the town as

destitute of beauty. . . . The inhabitants [are] principally farmers; sober, industrious, orderly citizens; not remarkable for energy; and, like those of East-Haven, less attentive than most of their countrymen to the

The Stony Creek shore

education of their children. A considerable number of them are seamen, and are principally employed by the merchants of New Haven. . . . Branford appears as if it has already arrived at a stand in the progress of improvement, and had become fixed in its present state by a mere want of energy and effort.

New Englanders used to say with a rueful humor (and a glance at their stone walls) that rocks were the most bounteous harvest of their fields. The development of the granite industry after 1850 made this literally true. The industry was favored in places like Stony Creek not only because they

19

had unique outcroppings of high-quality granite, but also because their seaside locations made it easy and cheap to transport this unusually heavy cargo. Before the advent of steel rails, bridges, and rolling stock, transporting loads of any great weight or size by rail was both expensive and hazardous.

In the decades following the Civil War, Stony Creek's rugged seaside landscape—and that of dozens of similarly situated rural villages throughout New England—was dramatically transformed. "The practice of quarrying consists in uncovering a sufficient surface of the rock by removing superficial soil," explained a turn-of-the-century writer, "and then with proper tools or, if necessary, with explosives, detaching blocks of form or size adapted to the purpose in view."

In short order, places where forests once grew and cows and sheep once grazed were stripped of their natural coverings and turned into wastelands of rock shards, dust, smoke, and noise. Hillsides disappeared. ("A quarry should," the writer urged, "be opened on a hillside.") Towering wooden derricks, guyed with heavy rope or steel cable, moved blocks of stone from quarry faces to work sheds for cutting and finishing, and then to railroad flatcars or schooners and barges for transport to construction sites throughout the Northeast.

Near the quarries, ramshackle boardinghouses provided food and shelter for the armies of men, skilled and unskilled, needed to pursue "the art of winning or obtaining from the earth's crust the various kinds of stone used in construction." Sometimes the dwellings were so close to quarrying operations that fragments of stone dislodged by blasting peppered roofs and broke windows.

Large-scale use of granite as a building material began as early as the 1820s, when Boston merchants began quarrying operations at Quincy, south of the city. They sought material to construct the Bunker Hill Monument and to help in the process of turning their fire-prone city into a city of brick and stone. But it would be many years before granite was commonly used by American builders and monument makers. Weight aside, the major obstacle to granite's general use was the difficulty of working it. While it was fairly easy to use hand tools on granite—working with the natural rift and grain of the stone to cut it into rough blocks for foundations and paving stones—it was quite another matter to cut and finish the "rock of ages." Until the widespread use of tools powered by steam (1840s) and compressed air (1870s) and the availability of reasonably priced, high-grade steel (1870s), architects, engineers, masons, and

Railroad tracks and derrick in the quarry, August 1906

monument makers preferred marble and sandstone over granite. These softer stones were simply easier to work.

A MARKET FOR GRANITE

In 1848, New Haven stonecutters Thomas Phillips and Treat Botsford purchased property at the corner of High and Grove Streets, opposite the entry to the Grove Street Cemetery. Their deed mentioned that their stone and marble works would use "machinery to be driven by a steam engine . . . in the business of sawing, sanding, polishing, and turning marble or stone." Phillips had been the head designer and carver for New Haven's leading stonecutting family, the Ritters, and his new firm combined state-of-the-art technology with remarkable artistry. In the process, it quickly attracted prestigious commissions for stonework in new homes and public buildings and for cemetery monuments. Phillips & Botsford soon asserted its uniqueness among the city's artisans: Where others used sandstone and marble, Phillips & Botsford used granite. It was not long after the new firm's establishment that B.N. Green, the New London stonecutter who set up the first quarry in the Stony Creek section of Branford, began to appear regularly in the Phillips company's ledgers as a supplier of granite. By the 1880s, Phillips had

surpassed Ritters—New Haven's oldest stone carvers, whose *forte* was sandstone—as the region's premiere stoneworks, a position it would retain for the next century.

Thomas Phillips was not an inventor or innovator. He was an entrepreneur with a keen eye for inventions and innovations that would give him an edge over his competitors. By the 1840s, he was subscribing to international trade journals and purchasing pattern books published in Paris and London that showed the latest fashions in monumental design and the architecture of public and private buildings. These not only enabled him to market the latest styles and motifs, but gave him access to the new tools and methods that were making it possible to work with materials like granite. By the 1860s, the hallmarks of Phillips's monumental work were granite tombstone bases. By the 1880s, strategically placed advertisements called New Haveners' attention to "Phillips Steam, Marble, Granite, and Stone Works." By the 1890s, he had largely relegated his marble work to the basement of his workshop and was working entirely in granite. With tools powered by compressed air, his growing workforce of German, Irish, and Italian carvers was able to fashion exquisitely detailed monuments and architectural elements from a material that came

22

in an amazing variety of colors and textures and whose hardness defied time itself.

Thomas Phillips's success did not depend only on technology, however. The mere availability of granite did not assure its acceptance. Cities were growing and changing, and with them the culture and economy of the nation. The growth of the granite market owed much to transformations that had little to do with the material itself.

Increased investments in *urban infrastructures* led to the paving of streets and sidewalks, for example, and city managers greatly increased the construction of bridges, piers, jetties, tunnels, sewer systems, and waterworks. At the same time, *public safety* became a growing concern. Nineteenth-century cities were prone to disastrous fires, which spread rapidly among wooden structures, often destroying whole neighborhoods. In the last third of the century, cities began to adopt strict building and fire codes that mandated the use of brick and stone in construction.

Investments in *public buildings* grew, as well. In the decades following the Civil War, the expanding scope and scale of government activity at all levels found expression in extravagant building projects. Harbor fortifications, lighthouses, piers, jetties, courthouses, state capitols and city halls, schools, prisons, hospitals, almshouses, and asylums rose in towns and cities throughout the country. Some were built entirely of granite. Many others used granite foundations, steps, and ornamental accents. Contracts for these public works represented vital currency for politicians in the corrupt and intensely partisan Gilded Age.

The new industrial enterprises of the post-Civil War decades dwarfed anything that had existed in the past. And these, in turn, produced *personal fortunes* of immense size, which were used to build enormous houses and sprawling estates. To the extent of their ability, the middle classes emulated the new captains of industry, constructing homes in an amazing assortment of styles and using many different materials. Granite—with its variety of colors and textures and capacity to be worked into almost any motif a designer could imagine—proved to be a material particularly suited to expressing both the aspirations of the well-to-do and the civic pride of growing cities. The desire to celebrate in stone the achievements of families, private institutions, and governments did not stop with the creation of mansions and imposing institutional edifices. It extended to memorials of past achievements, both in cemetery monuments and in prominently placed public art.

Works in progress that required the labor of a skilled carver

Meanwhile, the arrival of *a great wave of immigrants* produced an unprecedented labor force. The economic and political turbulence of the second half of the nineteenth century brought millions of immigrants, skilled and unskilled, to American shores. Among the newcomers from Italy and Scandinavia were workers trained in the latest techniques of quarrying and stone carving, with experience in using such new technologies as drills and other stoneworking tools powered by compressed air. Stoneworking was a skilled craft, and the numbers of available skilled workers enabled American quarrymen to employ large crews at relatively low costs. The historic craft traditions of these same stoneworkers, however, would lay the foundation for fierce resistance to employers' efforts to exploit them. Stoneworkers were eventually numbered among the best and most effectively organized groups of workers in the United States.

What ultimately made the market for granite "take off" was not local demand from entrepreneurs like Phillips, but *national demand* on a huge scale, with the transcontinental railroad as a means to serve it. The orders of small businessmen could not drive the expansion of the market, but huge contracts could—for projects such as the Brooklyn Bridge, the Statue of Liberty, and countless public buildings throughout the land.

Because the architectural fashions of the time demanded *varieties of materials,* firms that could contract to supply wide ranges of materials, preferably in finished form, won the day. As a result, the small backyard quarries of the 1850s and 1860s soon gave way to national or regional dealerships with offices in New York, Boston, or Washington. The labor force mirrored the character of the market. Extended families of stoneworkers settled in major quarrying centers; workers and their families moved from quarry to quarry, according to where the jobs were; and the labor organizations that protected their interests became some of the earliest national unions. Not surprisingly, names familiar to residents of a community such as Stony Creek would appear in period trade publications located in Massachusetts, on the granite islands of Maine's Penobscot Bay, or in Vermont's Barre region.

—PDH

ROCK FARMS

The story of the granite quarries has a large and varied cast of characters. The quarries would not have existed without the builders and architects who demanded hewn stone. Neither would they have been able to operate without the workforce—strong and willing, skilled or not—that arrived from foreign parts. But all these players ultimately depended on the brave souls who envisioned an industry and took the financial risk to open the hard earth itself as a business venture.

GREEN'S QUARRY

On July 1, 1852, the first train of the Shore Line Railroad chugged its way through Stony Creek. The route of this one-track railroad ran near the shore of Long Island Sound and among the rich granite resources of the area.

The first quarryman to take advantage of this situation was Benjamin Green, who had quarry interests in Mystic and Groton. Green and his nephew purchased land at the present Hall's Point between the Sound and the railroad in 1858 and opened a quarry there the next year. He was able to ship his granite by sea or rail. At its height, the quarry employed about 50 workers. While most of these men were native of the northeastern United States, several came from Ireland.

In the 1860s, Mr. Green suffered a severe accident. An early history states that "by the premature discharge of a blast in his quarry he was laid aside." Green moved to New Haven, and his nephew, Guy Turner, operated the quarry. By 1869, Green had purchased a railroad sidetrack in New Haven and opened a granite stone yard on the corner of Grove and High Streets, across from the gate of the Grove Street Cemetery. He advertised that he could now fill orders for monuments, building stones, and cemetery work of all kinds on short notice. Two examples of his cemetery monuments exist in the Damascus Cemetery near Stony Creek. They honor the Barker and Howd families, both of whom lived near the quarry.

Tragedy again struck the quarry when Guy Turner died of pneumonia in 1874 at the age of 43. His estate was unable to keep the quarry, and it was closed and the land sold.

A probate inventory of the estate reveals land in Stony Creek and New Haven, a storehouse, barn, blacksmith shop, derricks, oxen and horses, millstone stock, cut posts, sills, steps, brace posts, cut basin heads, 1,046 paving blocks, cemetery markers, finished cemetery monuments, and many other items of stock and equipment.

GRANITE ISLAND QUARRY

The second commercial quarry in Stony Creek was located on Rogers Island in the Thimble Islands, not far offshore from Green's Quarry. The quarry was opened in 1862 by Constant Webb of Wallingford under the name of the Granite Island Quarry. Webb leased the island for 15 years at an annual rent of $150 plus 2 cents per cubic foot for dimensional stone and 10 cents a ton for other stone that was removed.

The operation erected a boardinghouse on the island, which in 1870 housed two overseers from New York and Maine and 10 stonecutters— one each from New York, Holland, and England, two each from Connecticut and Ireland, and three from Scotland. The quarry inhabitants also included one local stone mason, three local seamen, one Irish and two English blacksmiths, and five women.

On April 17, 1870, the boardinghouse burned to the ground but was soon rebuilt. At this time,

the quarry had a contract to provide granite for St. Mary's Church on Hillhouse Avenue in New Haven. Although much of the structure is built of trap rock from West Rock in New Haven, the window- and doorjambs, sills, strings, belts, water tables (projecting courses that threw off rainwater), and quoins (exterior angles) are of Stony Creek granite. Of note are the pink bands on the door surrounds. The church was completed in 1874.

The quarry struggled financially, and Philander Hopson placed a lien against the company. Granite Island Quarry had failed to pay Hopson for building a boarding and dwelling house on the island. Lease payments ceased, and the island reverted to the owners (who had both died) in 1879.

Another small quarry operation was also opened on a neighboring island. In 1870, Thomas Pearson of New York purchased Goat Island (later Bear Island) and quarried granite that was used for bridges across the Connecticut River at Saybrook, Middletown, and Hartford.

PINE ORCHARD QUARRY

The Pine Orchard Quarry was opened at Juniper Point to the west of Stony Creek in 1870. Because the water abutting the quarry was shallow, the quarry sought to put a

Schooner at Pine Orchard breakwater (far left)

Flying Point Hotel (near left)

causeway out to a nearby island but had to settle for a long dock with tracks on it for loading granite.

Although the Pine Orchard Quarry produced paving stones for New York, its major contract was to furnish granite to rebuild Fort Diamond in New York. Fort Diamond had been built on a 2.5-acre (1-hectare) reef about 200 yards (182.9 m) off the Brooklyn shore of the Narrows in 1812. Renamed Fort Lafayette in 1823 in honor of the French military hero, the Marquis de Lafayette, and his visit to the United States, the structure had 8-foot (2.4-meter) thick walls rising 30 feet (9.1 m) and mounted 73 guns in three tiers.

On December 1, 1868, the fort went up in flames. Fireboats and tugs attempted to halt the fire to no avail. When the firefighters realized that the fort held large amounts of explosives, they fled. At this time, dwellings within a half-mile (0.8 km) radius of the fort along the Brooklyn shore were evacuated. Several years later, the fort was rebuilt with granite from the Pine Orchard Quarry. In 1960, the site of the fort was used as one of the supports for the Verrazano-Narrows Bridge.

The Pine Orchard Quarry ran into financial difficulties and was disbanded and sold to the Doolittle family in 1878.

RED HILL/
STONY CREEK RED GRANITE QUARRY

In 1874, F.W. Redpath of Plymouth, Massachusetts, opened a quarry under the name of the Connecticut Granite Company for the purpose of supplying granite for the Metropolitan Museum of Art in New York City's Central Park. Located about a mile and a half (2.4 km) north of the center of Stony Creek in the Red Hill area, the quarry provided granite for the statehouses in Hartford and Albany in 1876. Under New York ownership, it became the Red Hill Quarry and was later named the Stony Creek Red Granite Quarry.

Most of this quarry's products were used for building purposes in the New York City area. The operation's sole access to Long Island Sound, which provided transportation to New York City, was a railroad sidetrack. Much to the dismay of summer visitors and residents, in 1890, the quarry purchased the Island View Hotel and its dock on Flying Point. The hotel became the quarry headquarters, the dock was enlarged, and a cutting department, granite sheds, and shipping wharf were added.

In the mid-1890s, the quarry was temporarily abandoned. In 1898, it reopened, but with sporadic success. At that time, the plant had six

27

NEW HAVEN RAILROAD 222
(LATER 2136)
Photographed in New Rochelle, NY, on August 13, 1903 (inset), the engine was originally used in shuttle passenger service. In March 1906, the engine was sold to the Red Granite Co. of Stony Creek (right).

28

derricks, two hoisting engines, a locomotive, three steam drills, an air compressor, eight plug drills, 12 air hand tools, and a surfacer.

In 1922, the Dodds Granite Company, which had held the quarry mortgage, foreclosed and obtained the quarry. At that time, the quarry held 26 pieces of real estate, tools, machinery, sailing vessels, implements, franchises, rights, scows, steam vessels, and other apparatus and equipment. The hotel was not included and eventually returned to its former use.

BRANFORD RIVER QUARRIES

In 1880, work was begun on the construction of three granite breakwaters off New Haven Harbor. Two quarries were leased on the Branford River to furnish stone for this project. The Graham-Roddin Quarry consisted of a 50-foot (15.2-meter) granite cliff on the river where the present Sylvan Point complex is located. The Lanphier Quarry was at Lanphier's Cove on the river.

In 1881, the quarries were worked by 50 or 60 Swedes who had formerly worked at Beattie's Quarries. It was within the Branford River quarries that the largest blast ever set in Branford occurred in 1883. Workers drilled five holes 20 feet (6.1 m) deep and located 15 feet (4.6 m) in back of a ledge that was 17 to 80 feet (5.2 to 24.4 m) long. Using 25 dynamite cartridges, they blew out between 200,000 and 300,000 tons (180,000 and 270,000 t) of solid stone.

The quarries used two old schooners to transport the granite. The schooners' masts were converted to derricks, and the side bulwarks were lowered to accommodate the granite. The two ships were then towed to the breakwater site. In this way, the operation could carry 100 tons (90 t) of stone per trip.

The breakwaters were not completed until the end of the century, employing numerous contractors.

QUARRIES AT THE PINES

Three quarries were located in an area called The Pines, in western Stony Creek, in the vicinity of Pine Creek and Route 146. Although these operations were short-lived and small to moderate in size, they deserve to be mentioned.

In about 1880, the Granite State Provident Company of New Hampshire opened a quarry.

In 1883, the company ran into "rotten rock," and the quarry was abandoned. In 1886, John Hanna of New Britain, who also owned a quarry in Guilford, opened the Hanna Quarry, which operated at least until his death in 1896. In 1891, the Totokett Granite Company of New Jersey opened a quarry to extract stone for its pinkish color. A rail spur enabled all three quarries to transport their products via the railroad.

NORCROSS BROTHERS/DODDS/ CASTELLUCCI QUARRY

In 1887, contractors from Worcester, Massachusetts, called Norcross Brothers opened a large quarry in Stony Creek about a mile and a quarter (2 km) north of the village. The company was a large-scale builder of public buildings, private residences, educational structures, business blocks, churches, and railroad stations. They were often associated with the architect H.H. Richardson (1838–1886). One of the first buildings to use granite from this quarry was Osborn Hall (built in 1888 and razed in 1926) on a corner of Yale's Old Campus. A long list of buildings and monuments throughout the United States and abroad followed (see "Stony Creek granite on the rise," page 30). The operation used a railroad spur that ran from the quarry to the main railroad line.

Stony Creek granite on the rise

As part of their promotion material in the company's heyday, Castellucci & Sons, Inc., offered Stony Creek pink granite's impressive resumé to potential buyers. "Nature's most wonderful and individual stone," they announced. "Non-staining and eternally beautiful." As a sales piece, their description of the stone is compelling and the list of prominent buildings impressive. As a historical document, the list portrays a more fundamental phenomenon—the impact of one small, regional business on a thriving national scene.

CASTELLUCCI & SONS, INC.
PARTIAL LIST OF PROMINENT
BUILDINGS ERECTED IN STONY
CREEK GRANITE

Hudson River Bridge, Ft. Washington, NY, to Ft. Lee, NJ, Cass Gilbert, Architect
Whitney Central Bank, New Orleans, LA
Harris Trust & Savings Bank, Monroe Street, Chicago, IL
Conn. Gen. Life Ins. Co. Building, Hartford, CT, James Gamble Rogers, Architect
Grand Central Station, New York City
Pershing Square Building, New York City, York & Sawyer & John Sloan, Associates, Architects
Newberry Library, Chicago, IL

Central Railway of New Jersey Building, New York City
Head House Philadelphia & Reading, RR, Philadelphia, PA
R.H. Macy & Co. Bldg., 34th St. & Broadway, New York City
New York Telephone Building, New York City, McKenzie, Voorhees & Gmelin, Architects. Barclay-Vesey, Washington & West Sts.
No. 2 Park Avenue Building, New York City
Lefcourt Manhattan Building, 39th St. & Broadway, New York City
Columbia University Buildings, New York City
Barnard College, New York City
South Terminal Station, Boston, MA
Bellevue Hospital, New York City
Grosvenor Building, Providence, RI
War College, Washington, D.C.
Provident Savings Bank, Baltimore, MD
Greenwich Savings Bank Building, 36th St. & Broadway, New York City
Rochester Savings Bank, Rochester, NY, McKim, Mead & White, Architects
Lincoln Alliance Bank, Rochester, NY, McKim, Mead & White, Architects
Warren Trust & Savings Bank, Warren, PA, Hopkins & Dentz, Architects
Philadelphia Savings Fund Society, Philadelphia, PA
Shelburne Hotel, Atlantic City, NJ, Warren & Wetmore, Architects

Bulkeley Bridge over Connecticut River, Hartford, CT
Y.M.C.A. Building, Worcester, MA
Masonic Temple, Springfield, OH
Guardian Savings & Trust Company Building, Cleveland, OH
Jersey City Trust Co. Building, Jersey City, NJ, Clinton & Russell, Architects
Beacon Journal Co. Building, Akron, OH, Allen & DeYoung, Architects
Hadley Falls Trust Co. Building, Holyoke, MA, McKim, Mead & White, Architects
Leonard Building, New Britain, CT
First National Bank Building, Columbus, IN
Bender Building, Montreal, Canada
Boss Building, New London, CT
Branigan Building, Providence, RI
Broadway Franklin Building, New York City
East Liverpool Bank Columns, East Liverpool, OH
Elks' Building, Bridgeport, CT
Empire Building Columns, Birmingham, AL
Fall River Church, Fall River, MA
Fulton Building, Pittsburgh, PA
Hammond Laboratory, Yale University, New Haven, CT
Hampden Hospital, Springfield, MA
Hartford High School, Hartford, CT
Hippodrome Building, New York City
Ladd's School of Mines, New York City

Morton Residence, New York City

New England Telephone Building, Hartford, CT

North Easton Bank, North Easton, MA

Rochester German Insurance Building, Rochester, NY

South Norwalk Bank, Norwalk, CT

Stevens Building, Providence, RI

Third National Bank, Cumberland, MD

Waterbury Station, Waterbury, CT

Broadway Chambers Building, New York City

Chelsea Piers, Base Course, New York City

Hallenback-Hungerford Building, New York City

Lord & Taylor Base Course, 38th St. & 5th Ave., New York City

S.W. Straus Building, 5th Ave. & 46th St., New York City

Arsenal Building, 463 7th Ave., New York City

Powers Building, 723 7th Ave., New York City

Schwarzenbach Building, 470 4th Ave., New York City

Astor House, 217 Broadway, New York City

Underwood Building, 28 Vesey St., New York City

Insurance Center Building, John, Gold & Platte Sts., New York City

Delmonico Building, 44th St. & 5th Ave., New York City

Mills & Gill Building, 288 4th Ave., New York City

Office Building, 65 W. 39th St., New York City

Office Building, 12 E. 44th St., New York City

Office Building, 37th St. & 6th Ave., New York City

Office Building, 39th & 6th Ave., New York City

Office Building, 15–19 E. 33rd St., New York City

Office Building, 213 E. 37th St., New York City

Loft Building, 35th St. & 7th Ave., New York City

Loft Building, 39th St. & 7th Ave., New York City

Apartment Building, 50–56 W. 96th St., New York City

Apartment Building, 68th St. & Madison Ave., New York City

Dixie Terminal Building, Cincinnati, OH

Fulton National Bank, Lancaster, PA

Summit Trust Company Building, Summit, NJ

Some jobs under construction or recently completed in Stony Creek granite

Smithsonian Institute, Museum of History & Technology, Washington, D.C., McKim, Mead & White, Architects

American Mutual Life Ins. Co., Wakefield, MA, Chester Lindsey Churchill, Architect

Eastern Air Lines Terminal, Idlewild Airport, New York City, Chester Lindsey Churchill, Architect

Telephone Building, New Haven, CT, Douglas Orr, Architect

First New Haven National Bank, New Haven, CT, Douglas Orr, Architect

Columbia University, New York, City, Shreve, Lamb & Harmon, Architects

St. John's Seminary, Brighton, MA, Joseph Gregory McGann, Architect

New England Conservatory of Music, Boston, MA, Kilham, Hopkins, Greeley & Brodee, Architects

Whitney National Bank, New Orleans, LA, Goldstein, Parham & Labouisse, Architects

Harris Trust & Savings Bank, Chicago, IL, Skidmore, Owings & Merrill, Architects

First Safe Deposit National Bank, New Bedford, MA, Hutchins & French, Architects

Eight House, Harvard University, Boston, MA, Shepley, Bulfinch, Richardson & Abbott, Architects

In 1900, Norcross Brothers employed 200 men, half of whom were expert stonecutters. In 1910, the plant owned 11 derricks; 11 hoisting engines; an overhead traveling crane of 20 tons (18 t); eight hand derricks; two locomotives; a 30-horsepower dynamo for polishers, lathes, and lighting; five steam drills; two air compressors; 14 air plug drills; 15 air hand tools; five surfacers; a gang of saws; two sets of double-pendulum polishers; three polishing lathes; and steam pumps.

In 1923, the Dodds Granite Company of Milford, Massachusetts, purchased the quarry for $128,000. The quarry remained active until 1929; ownership was retained.

In 1955, the Castellucci family, with quarry interests in Providence, Rhode Island, purchased the quarry and reopened it. Their markets were mainly in Boston, New York City, and Washington, D.C. The business flourished in the 1960s but went downhill in the 1970s. In 1977, Castellucci sold the quarry land of 405 acres (162 ha) to the Town of Branford; 50 acres (20 ha) were to be leased back for further quarrying. In 1979, architect Philip Johnson chose Stony Creek granite to face his New York City American Telephone and Telegraph Company Building, an 11-million-dollar contract. After this short-lived prosperity, business declined, despite five buildings for a Cleveland clinic by Cesar Pelli, a building and additions for the Bristol-Meyers Squibb Research Center in nearby Wallingford, and the buildings Four Times Square and the New York Mercantile Exchange in Manhattan.

BROOKLYN QUARRY

The Brooklyn Quarry was opened in 1889 by the Branford Granite Company, a business composed of Brooklyn investors. Contrary to local legend, the Brooklyn Quarry had nothing to do with the Brooklyn Bridge, which had opened six years earlier. Located in the southeastern part of Stony Creek, near Long Island Sound, this quarry produced a grayish granite that was used for paving stones and for bridges and breakwaters.

The Brooklyn Quarry closed in 1895 but reopened two years later on a reduced scale. In 1910, a stone crusher was brought in from Guilford, and the quarry's stone was used for a trolley roadbed intended to run from Branford to Guilford. By 1919, the quarry had closed and the Bullard family bought the site for a summer complex.

—JBK

32

BEATTIE'S QUARRIES

John Beattie was a Scotsman, strong and robust, with a sharp business acumen and a love of the outdoors. His quarries, located in the Leete's Island District of Guilford, probably constituted one of the largest industrial enterprises of the era along the south shore of Connecticut. He fulfilled contracts from New York to Boston, including those for hotel plazas, railroad bridges, beacons, breakwaters, lighthouses, and even a grain elevator.

Like most of the late nineteenth-century quarry proprietors, John Beattie's fortunes waxed and waned, but unlike many of his competitors, he enjoyed a widespread reputation. It was Beattie who received the government contract to supply every granite block in the pedestal of the Statue of Liberty (1884–1886). Other American icons quarried from the Beattie's Quarries include North Lighthouse on Block Island and the Brooklyn Bridge abutments in New York.

John Beattie was born in Edinburgh, Scotland, in 1821. As a child, he emigrated to Canada with his parents, where his father carried on his trade of stonemason and contractor in Halifax, Nova Scotia, and later, in Newport, Rhode Island. At age 13, John learned the fundamentals of stonecutting. Following a journey to California as a gold miner, he and his brother began their own business in Newport. In 1865, the brothers purchased a quarry in Fall River, Massachusetts, but John left to open his own quarry in Niantic, Connecticut.

Many of Beattie's contracts were in the New York area, and as he transported granite on Long Island Sound in his great schooners, he learned every indentation in the shoreline. He was scouting for bigger and better, and he found what he wanted. In February 1870, he purchased his first real estate in Guilford and Branford, an 18-acre (7.2-hectare) tract at Hoadley's Neck on the east end of the Stony Creek District, followed by another purchase of 60 contiguous acres (24 ha), straddling the town's boundary line. He renovated an old farmhouse on the edge of a snug harbor for his home and headquarters. This dwelling is now maintained by Yale University as a biology field station at 276 Old Quarry Road. Offshore, "No Man's Island" became his repository for black powder for explosives.

Before his death in 1899, John Beattie amassed 350-plus acres (140-plus ha) on Hoadley's Neck, including over 1 mile (1.6 km) of waterfront. The land was rough and untillable, crisscrossed with cliffs of ancient granite in hues of red, pink, and gray. Professor Herbert

33

Gregory of Yale University believed that Beattie's vein of Stony Creek/Leete's Island granite was the second hardest in the United States—second only to granites found in Montana and Wyoming. The supply seemed inexhaustible. As one quarry cliff was cut back, a new one was opened. There were West Quarry, Middle Quarry, and East Quarry right down on the waterfront of the point, and then, in about 1876, Beattie opened a new quarry north of the railroad line.

The late Robert Beattie (1898–1992), grandson of John Beattie, said that the "the Patch," as the quarry area came to be called, became a thriving community of its own. In its heyday, Beattie's operation employed about 500 people who lived in shacks, shanties, and boardinghouses sprinkled around the rocky hilltops. The quarry superintendents and schooner captains lived in the neat row of Victorian dwellings still standing in the No. 36–54 block of Old Quarry Road.

The town line separating Guilford and Branford passed through the middle of John Beattie's home and bisected Hoadley's Point, leading to confusion regarding town taxation and electoral privileges. Mr. Beattie variously petitioned to have the line altered to put all of his holdings in either one town or the other. Finally,

in 1885, the Connecticut legislature reestablished the line at Hoadley's Creek, officially locating all of the Neck and all of Beattie's properties in the Leete's Island District of Guilford.

Like other quarry owners, Beattie drew his workforce from the tide of immigrants who came to America in the 1880s and 1890s. Chiefly Irish, Finns, and Swedes, as well as Italians and Scots, they labored together to produce, among other structures, the base for the greatest symbol of American freedom, the Statue of Liberty.

One group of Hungarian workers, hard rock miners from the Old Country, entered employment at Beattie's Quarries under the mistaken belief that Beattie operated mines. The workers stayed, however, and learned the ways of open quarrying. A religious group that could not bring their ritual implements with them, the group carved their religious vessels—including a monstrance and chalice—in a ledge along the Patch Road. At this rock altar, they performed religious services.

Robert Beattie reminisced that the quarrymen with European backgrounds relished meals of fresh eels. "At low tide," he writes, "it was common to see a dozen men out along [Hoadley's] creek bank stabbing away with their long-handled eel spears." They also skinned the eels for their thin, strong, pliable leather, which

could be stretched on broom handles for seasoning. The skins would be laid out on the blacksmith shop vise, and then cut into strips with razor blades and made into shoelaces that never broke.

Mr. Beattie's labor force consisted of a field crew in addition to the quarry work crew. Convenient access to Long Island Sound made shipments via schooner fast and economical. Beattie maintained a full fleet of sturdy sailing vessels for this part of the operation. The most famous of them was the *Wasp*, a Hudson River sloop built in 1813, that would later serve as a privateer for the duration of the War of 1812 (which ended in 1815). When Beattie purchased the *Wasp* in 1871, she was fitted with a long derrick boom and a steam hoisting engine with a boiler that stood in the hold. Due to her broad beam, the *Wasp* was commissioned to carry the four largest stones on the Statue of Liberty job— the door lintels—each weighing 7 tons (6.3 t).

After nearly 50 years of prosperity, Beattie's

35

Hughes Brothers and Bangs Quarry, Sachem's Head, circa 1909

Quarries suspended operations. In the era of World War I, overhead costs skyrocketed, especially the bulk purchase of coal, gunpowder, and steel. Many of the skilled Scottish quarrymen returned to England to serve in the military reserves. The sons of the late John Beattie went into bankruptcy. John Beattie's probate estate remained open 45 years, until the final sale of real estate in 1945. Premier waterfront homes in the private Old Quarry Association now stand like sepulchral markers over the quarry that has earned rank and honor in the annals of Connecticut industrial history.

HUGHES BROTHERS AND BANGS QUARRY

Across the shore from the site of Beattie's Quarries, across Island Bay and Great Harbor, a large jutting promontory known as Uncas Point forms the north side of Sachem's Head Harbor. Today it is a flat landscape with modern homes—in stark contrast to the 60-foot (18.3-meter) bluff that was obliterated by former quarry operations. But 120 years ago, it was the site of the Hughes Brothers and Bangs Quarry. Although in scope of operation and quality of stone, the Hughes Brothers and Bangs Quarry was no match for Beattie's, it supplied a significant amount of riprap for construction of breakwaters and retaining walls.

High on the original bluff of this point, the decapitated head of a Pequot Indian chief, or *sachem,* was placed in the crotch of an oak tree during the Pequot Indian War. This grizzly event, which christened Sachem's Head as a geographic place name, occurred in 1637—two years before the founding of Guilford.

The first quarry venture at Uncas Point, when it was known as Caldwell's Point, is recorded in the Guilford Land Records in 1871. Darwin Benton leased 11 acres (4.4 ha) "intended for a granite quarry" to one Asa Cady Palmer of Fayetteville, New York. Palmer's local representative was William W. Lee, who was subcontracted by Beattie's Quarries to supply part of the stone for the granite work in the tunnel in New York City, from the Harlem River to Grand Central Depot (1873–1875).

By 1887, the firm of Allen and Comey conducted quarry operations at Uncas Point. Hughes Brothers and Bangs, headquartered in Syracuse, New York, purchased a large section of the point during the years from 1894 to 1896. By the turn of the century, the quarry was booming with up to 150 laborers, mostly Italian, who lived in little shacks and dugouts in the quarry itself. Bunkhouses in the wreck of an old sailing vessel, beached on the shore of Great Harbor, also served as living accommodations.

The workers faced the worst kind of deprivations and referred to their workplace as "Abyssinia" in unpleasant remembrance of African Abyssinia (Ethiopia), where Italy had waged a war a few years earlier.

Hughes Brothers and Bangs Quarry had a working face of granite about 1,000 feet (305 m) long, accessed by a system of locomotive tracks converging at the stone shipping wharf. The operation used 14 derricks of 10 tons (9 t) each and custom-built, A-frame derrick barges to haul the stone. Acquiring fresh water always posed a problem. After quickly depleting a dug reservoir, the quarry operators experimented using salt water in the steam plant boiler, with disastrous results. Scale deposits built up, and the overheated furnace exploded, killing a workman. Thereafter, water was pumped from a supply pond in Leete's Island, carried under the bay through a 3-inch (7.6-centimeter) steel pipe.

The summer cottagers on the other side of Sachem's Head Harbor found the quarry activity on Uncas Point irksome. Aside from the incessant blasting, which sent clouds of dust through the air, they complained about another annoying source of noise—the mockingbird locomotive whistle used to warn men off the tracks. Furthermore, dirt piles spilled into the

water and polluted their swimming beaches. Yet another controversy arose when sluicing operations used to expose new ledge uncovered the grave of an English sailor.

The Breakwater Construction Company of New York operated the Uncas Point quarry under bankruptcy after 1908. A Cleveland, Ohio, corporation took over, only to repeat the failure, resulting in the final downfall of the quarry by 1911.

TOOMEY BROTHERS QUARRY

One of Guilford's more obscure quarries operated at a single knoll of ledge off Route 146 on the approach to Leete's Island. In 1887, Humphrey Toomey purchased a narrow tract of woodland here bounded on its north by the old Shore Line Railroad and on its south by Leete's Island Road.

Humphrey and his brothers, Daniel and Dennis, were among the six children of Irish Catholic immigrants who came to New York City, and eventually to Beattie's Quarries, to learn a trade. By 1895, they operated their own quarry under power of a double-cylinder steam engine. They incorporated as a joint stock corporation in 1901.

The brothers specialized in the marine construction business, shipping stone by railroad

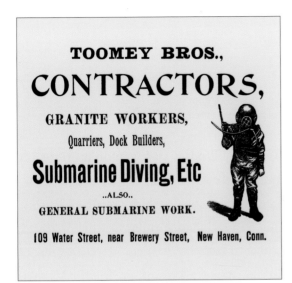

and fulfilling contracts for their specialty: lighthouses. Their office was located at 109 Water Street, New Haven, where one of their advertisements refers to "submarine diving" and "general submarine work."

Toomey Brothers built its first lighthouses at Narragansett Bay, Rhode Island (Plum Beach Light), and New Haven, Connecticut (Outer Break Wall Light), in 1899. These structures were built of iron in the caisson style, requiring hundreds of tons of riprap stone to prevent scouring around submerged bases. The caisson lighthouses were ballasted with concrete and towed to the site, making for a perilous water journey, even in the best of conditions. After pumping out sand and mud that had settled on the bottom of the lighthouse shoal, workers sunk an iron cylinder there, upon which they added living quarters.

The Toomeys owned a 105-foot (32-meter), two-masted schooner, designed as a floating workshop for jobs they contracted for in the

Chesapeake Bay area. Among their contracts were Hooper Island Lighthouse in Maryland (1900), Point No Point Lighthouse in Maryland (1902), and Peck's Light Ledge in Connecticut (1906). The Toomey Brothers operation was plagued by weather-related accidents, finally resulting in large financial loss and bankruptcy by 1909.

SAWPIT QUARRY

What may have been the first commercial granite quarry in the towns of Guilford and Branford is located on a hummock of ledge in the salt meadows embraced by East Creek and East River near the Madison town line. Now owned by the State of Connecticut, the site is part of the area known as "Saw Pit," so named because the first settlers used the area for hand-sawing logs with pit saws.

Rev. Henry Whitfield, Guilford's founder and spiritual leader, was the first to own the 160-acre (64-hectare) "Sawpitt Lot." At the time of the American Revolution, Wyllys Eliot owned and farmed the lot. It was sold by his sons.

Minard LaFever (1798–1854) of New York City, an eclectic pioneer architect whose extensive practice included works in the revival styles—particularly Gothic—acquired a one-tenth interest in the Sawpit "stone or

39

granite quarry" in 1837. This coincides with the construction of Guilford's Christ Episcopal Church, built in stone from this quarry in Gothic revival style. LaFever was not only a self-taught architect, but a well-trained carpenter and experienced builder.

The Sawpit Quarry used a narrow causeway road through the meadow to reach Eliot's Wharf on the bank of East River. From here, the operation shipped stone in sailing vessels to New York job sites. The blue-gray granite from Sawpit Quarry proved to be very hard, and when polished, it took on a beautiful, dark finish. The Leake and Watts Orphan Asylum in the twelfth ward of New York City was built from this granite, as were other public buildings. Architect LaFever relinquished his ownership interest in the quarry in 1845.

Sawpit Quarry discontinued operation for many years until it was resurrected to supply granite for the foundation of the Catholic church at 161 Whitfield Street in Guilford in 1876. The late first selectman of Guilford, Leslie Dudley, whose grandfather, Henry Dudley, kept a milking herd of cows east of Sawpit Quarry, also did general contracting for stonework. As Les Dudley told it, Grandpa Dudley hauled stone to the new church site using two oxcarts. His worker, Bill Bush, loaded at Sawpit Quarry and

met Grandpa Dudley partway on his return from the church site with an empty cart. The two exchanged ox teams, with the result of Bush loading stone all day and Dudley driving a team all day.

In the 1880s and 1890s, during the Victorian building boom, Elisha Hart owned the quarry site, but apparently entered into lease agreements with various quarrymen and contractors, including Richard Barrett and Granville Fuller, both residents of South Union Street near the quarry. Sawpit Quarry supplied curbing, paving, capstones, and underpinning for many local construction projects.

The quarry experienced a second resurrection after 1929 when Joseph Testori, a mason/contractor, purchased the quarry lot. Testori eventually worked in partnership with his son, Edward Sr. At first, they quarried stone for their own jobs, but during the building boom of the 1950s, they sold it by the square foot. A grandson, Edward Testori Jr., remembers going to the quarry as a boy to watch the drilling and blasting with dynamite. Manageable pieces of stone were turned on end with crowbars and finished with hand tools.

After about 125 years of periodic operation, Sawpit Quarry was permanently abandoned in the early 1960s.

HANNA'S QUARRY

In the heart of Guilford's West Woods, along the east side of the triangular meadow formerly known as Three Corner (Lost Lake), Hanna's granite quarry operated for about 20 years. The old road to Sachem's Head and Leete's Island, which is now the entrance to the West Woods trail system off Sam Hill Road, served as access.

John Hanna emigrated from Ireland and settled in New Britain, Connecticut, in 1858. He purchased 38 acres (15.2 ha) of rough woodland abutting the old Shore Line Railroad in 1888, establishing a north-south spur line, or sidetrack, for convenient transportation from the quarry ledges.

Little is known about Mr. Hanna's granite markets, but he is credited with the creation of the Tammany Regiment Monument in Gettysburg, Pennsylvania. As a sculptor and monumental architect, Mr. Hanna also advertised his services as a contractor and builder, with a showroom and office at 209 East Main Street, New Britain.

Today there are curious vestiges of the Hanna Quarry, all visible from the present-day nature trail marked as the "white trail." A narrow clearing crosses the trail, formerly used for the railroad sidetrack. A short distance beyond, next to the Amtrak rail corridor, an immense block of cut granite perches precariously on a high shelf of quarried ledge. Smaller cut blocks are strewn in piles.

Close to Lost Lake, the trail passes strange rock carvings that include a throne seat, pyramid with petals, flat rosette, unfinished Doric column, and rectangular trough. These stone "doodles" (see "A busman's holiday?", pages 42–43) raised ample speculation and brought a steady trail of tourists hoping, one would guess, for an exotic answer to the "mystery" of their origins.

—JEH

41

A busman's holiday?

What did a quarryman do at the end of his long workweek? Reports vary. For some, there was church on Sunday. Weekday meetings of the local union chapter or gatherings of amateur musicians could provide recreation. And the saloons promised camaraderie and a moment's forgetfulness. But for the occasional poorly paid quarryman, whose pocketbook was slim and whose work involved as much skill as muscle, the stone apparently never lost its charm. So we have learned since the first discovery of a collection of granite carvings a half-mile (0.8 km) into the West Woods of Guilford.

When hunters stumbled on the carvings in about 1930, they had no idea what they had found. One large rock had been shaped into what looked like a seat, complete with back and foot rest. Another stood about 18 inches (45.7 cm) tall, pyramid-shaped and decorated with overlapping rows of raised petals. Another rock, this one flat, had been patterned with large, four-petal flowers. And from a rock ledge appeared part of a Doric column, chiseled there as though to support some long-collapsed idea. The hunters carried news of their find to the community. From there, word spread and the speculations began.

Early on, an archaeologist named Charles Michael Boland arrived, equipped with an unlikely working theory. The Phoenicians had left their mark in these carvings, he suggested, probably sometime between 480 B.C.E. and 146 B.C.E. He believed that he had found other sites containing such relics in New Hampshire. He happily added the Guilford tracings to his list, including a colorful description of them in his book, *They All Discovered America:*

I can visualize the ship slowly probing the coast, perhaps putting into Leete's Island to repair a sail or damaged hull. Time was not important. The artisans aboard the ship whiled away their time by chiseling familiar figures in the rock. . . . The repairs finished, they left, their leisurely incisions in the rock silent evidence of their fleeting presence.

Boland's book generated more interest in the stone scribblings and brought other investigators and their theories into play. An archaeologist named William Flood decided to excavate a small portion of the site. When he and his son discovered clay potsherds that could be dated to Native American inhabitants of the region, their findings added weight to speculation that the carvings had their origins with the native peoples. But other investigators remained skeptical.

In the wake of the interest engendered by Boland's book in the early 1960s, the Guilford Free Library's librarian, Edith B. Nettleton, contacted an amateur archaeologist named Frank Glynn who had a fine reputation and "a passion for accuracy." His take on the carvings was less exotic, but no less intriguing.

The stonework, as he pointed out, was located on land that had been part of the quarry property owned by John Hanna. Glynn wrote:

I offered to give Boland detailed instructions for finding the carvings and gave him chapter and verse for the probability that the carvings are doodlings of the quarrymen, but he had a book to fill up. . . . [The carvings] were presumably done with modern tools and are located in amongst the outlines of the sheds and houses of the quarrymen. I have brought two competent sculptors in to look at [the carvings], and they are my authority for believing it is modern work with modern tools.

Quarry workers' descendants corroborate the idea that the carvings came from men whose livelihood resided in the selfsame stone. They remember stories told by mothers or uncles or grandfathers. They know that for some of the stoneworkers, the granite was more than work. It was a life.

Why in leisure would the quarrymen resort to doodling on the hard rock that bent their backs and filled their lungs with killing dust at work? Perhaps to test their tools or practice their carving skills. Perhaps simply to fill lonely hours with something that did not require spending their hard-earned pay. Or maybe, just maybe, the rock for some was not only the medium of their employment but of their passion, as well. Maybe, even after the long days of labor, they had visions of beauty in their minds and souls, and they used what they knew to express what they felt.

43

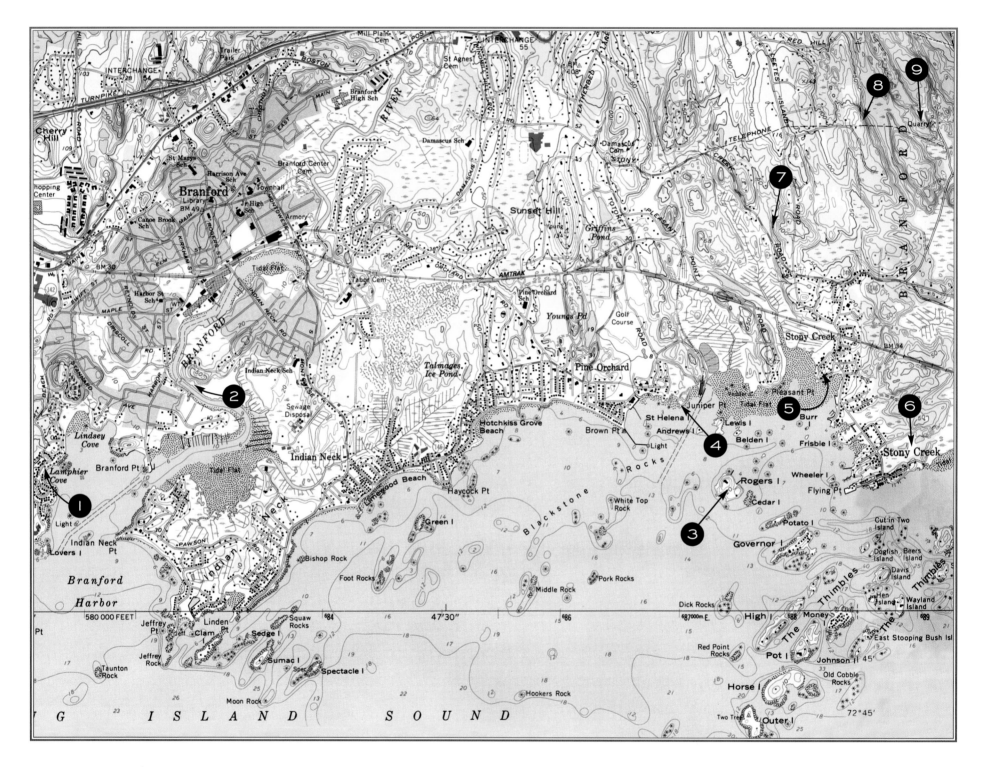

On the map

The 15 quarries located on the map operated for varying lengths of time during the height of the quarrying era.

1	LANPHIER QUARRY	6	BROOKLYN QUARRY
2	GRAHAM-RODDIN QUARRY	7	QUARRIES AT THE PINES
3	GRANITE ISLAND QUARRY	8	RED HILL/STONY CREEK RED GRANITE QUARRY
4	PINE ORCHARD QUARRY		
5	GREEN'S QUARRY	9	NORCROSS BROTHERS/DODDS/ CASTELLUCCI QUARRY

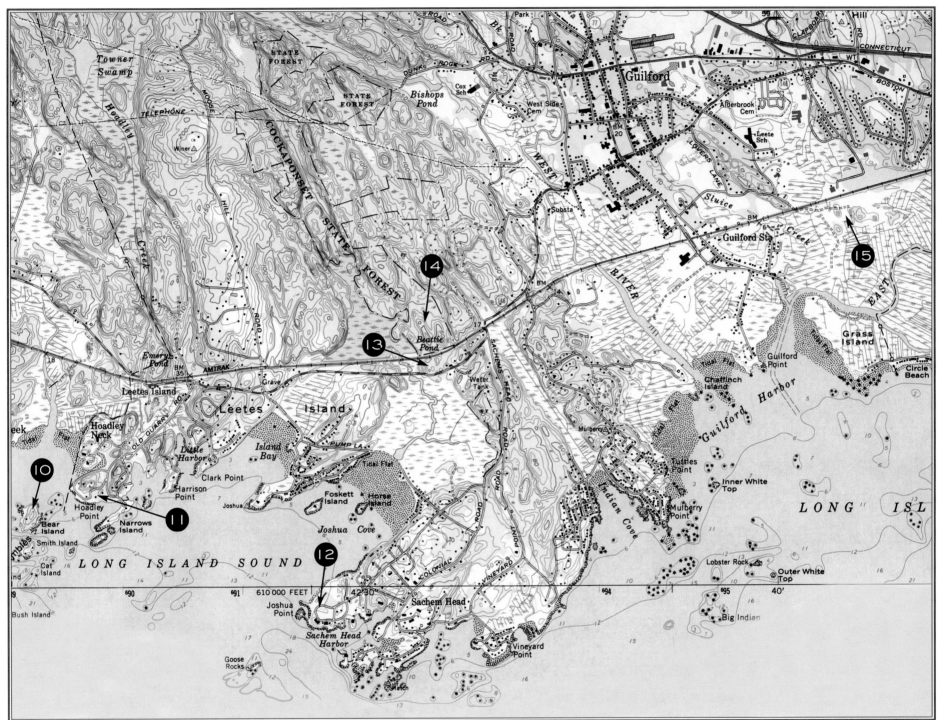

Map image courtesy of Maptech, Inc.

10   GOAT/BEAR ISLAND QUARRY

11   BEATTIE'S QUARRIES

12   HUGHES BROTHERS AND BANGS QUARRY

13   TOOMEY BROTHERS QUARRY

14   HANNA'S QUARRY

15   SAWPIT QUARRY

45

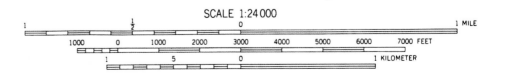

SCALE 1:24 000

There are three basic challenges that define the process of quarrying stone. The first involves freeing blocks of stone from bedrock or ledge. The second involves making the blocks of stone the desired size and shape. The third involves moving the blocks of stone to where they will be used. Advances in tools and technology to meet these three challenges have shaped the where and how of quarry work.

Until the nineteenth century, quarry work in the Stony Creek area mostly involved working an exposed face of ledge—of which there was more than adequate supply. The Reverend Henry Whitfield House in Guilford is believed to have been built in 1639 from gray granite that was taken from a ledge not far away from the house's eventual location. The blocks of stone used to build the house were extracted and cut by hand, and then transported across a marsh via a still discernable ridge of causeway that was probably built for just that purpose.

The hand method of extracting and sizing stone involved the use of a hand drill or a cross-pointed iron chisel, called a *star chisel,* to drill a row of 3-inch (7.6-centimeter) deep holes into the stone. Into each of these holes was placed a wedge-and-sleeve apparatus known as a *plug and feather.* If wedges alone are used to cleave stone, the force of the wedge is focused at the lip of the hole where the wedge is widest. This causes the surface of the stone to chip and flake—especially stone without a definite grain or proclivity. Placing a pair of iron pieces on either side of the wedge causes the face of the wedge to meet the inside surface of the hole more closely. In this way the pressure of the wedge is distributed deeper into the stone. The combined force of a row of these wedging sets drives a cleaving force deep enough into the stone to cause it to split with a loud crack.

The wedge piece of this apparatus was the *plug,* and the two pieces that married the plug to the hole were known as *feathers*—perhaps because of their tapered shape or the appearance of their horns sticking out of a hole. Plugs and feathers could vary in their shapes, but they were always matched to each other and to the shape of the hole formed by the drill.

A quarryman tapped each plug along the row of holes—working up and down the line—until the rock split. A skilled quarryman could sense the varying stress as he tapped each plug and tap it just enough to even out the force along the line. This method of splitting stone was so effective that it has remained the basis for quarrying—with some industrial enhancements—up to the present, although now it is used only for cutting stone, not extracting.

The private quarries—and even early commercial Stony Creek quarries, such as Green's Quarry, which opened in 1852 on Hall's Point Road, Goat Island Quarry (1860s on Bear Island), and Granite Island Quarry (1860s on Rogers Island)—most likely used this method. These early commercial quarries were small in scale, employing fewer than 50 workers. They tended to produce small blocks of stone—small enough to be carted on sledges or big-wheeled wagons drawn by oxen—and were located as close as possible to tidal waters to ease the transportation of the stone to its destination by boat.

—RD

SETTING WEDGES
Quarrymen drive wedges into the stone to split it.

Tools from Red Hill Quarry

circa late 1800s

Quarry workers used these tools both to quarry stone and to finish the stone once quarried.

blacksmith's hammer and tongs

Implements used by the many blacksmiths who were kept busy in the quarry, forging and sharpening tools

bush hammer

Hammers that have heads made up of many blades; used to cut down uneven surfaces of stone and produce a rough surface finish

chisel

Used for carved lettering and for smoothing rough places in the stone face, as well as for finer finishing work

feather

Flared pieces of iron that were sized to be placed in the holes made with the plug drills

level wedge

Placed in pairs on the surface of the stonework to support a straight edge between them, which then guided the leveling of the stone surface beneath

plug drill

Used to quarry the stone; hand drills were gradually replaced by steam drills, air drills, and ultimately, gas flame drills

point

Used for carved lettering and for smoothing rough places in the stone face

sledge hammer

In several sizes, used to strike the various cutting tools

wedge

Triangular piece of iron that was inserted in the feather and then tapped to drive the cut into the stone

EVOLVING POPULATION

THE IMMIGRANTS

The era that produced so unprecedented a burgeoning of both industry and immigration found "red-blooded Americans" screeching, "Foreigners, drunks, papists!" at the surge of newcomers to hit the shores of the United States. Immigration and the resultant swelling of a Roman Catholic population interacted, sometimes explosively, with the temperance and labor movements of the time. The granite quarries of the Stony Creek area played their part, however minuscule, both in bolstering and breaking down the intolerance, intemperance, and bigotry of the time. Battles, national and local, were not won easily or quickly.

In the decades leading up to the twentieth century, the temperance movement, calling for total abstinence in the use of alcoholic beverages, was at its zenith, propagated in the Protestant churches as eternal, unchanging dogma. At first, the temperance movement directed its energies almost solely at American Protestants. Then came the first influx of German and Irish immigrants who, as soon as they settled, opened their own churches and their own bars. Wherever they settled, saloons and *biergartens* soon followed, just at a time when the temperance movement was heating up. These foreigners came frolicking on the Sabbath at a time when strict Sabbath observance was taught and practiced in American Protestant communities.

Other immigrant groups followed in waves by the millions, invading a Protestant America that was intoxicated with its own moral, social, and economic power. Squalor, poverty, prostitution, labor unrest, violent strikes, and petty boss-ism ensued. Charges of papism, anarchy, and moral turpitude were hurled at the newcomers, many of whom did not speak English, most of whom were Roman Catholic, and all of whom were not American.

Religious leaders and social activists alike simplistically but correctly blamed social ills on alcohol and saloons. Women and families suffered especially the effects of drunken abuse, child neglect, and squandered paychecks. Yet women had no vote—on temperance issues

The original Protestant meeting house in Stony Creek (right). It burned to the ground in 1900 (far right).

or any other issues. In fact, the very saloons from which women were barred saw the consummation by powerful city bosses of many political decisions. The great and noble crusade for temperance—enormous in its influence within everyday Protestant thinking—became linked with women's rights, nativism, abolition, labor unions, evangelism, and other social reform movements.

In an environment where Protestant sensitivities and political traditions were under assault, cultures clashed at the most fundamental levels. While only extremists gave it voice, average Protestants looked at the rapid changes taking place throughout their society and suspected that the Vatican was, indeed, using immigration as part of a conspiracy to take over the country. Nativism, especially when bonded to temperance, fueled a strong bias against Roman Catholics and many immigrants.

As go the cities—where immigration typically has its first impact—so go the hamlets in time. The original Protestant meeting house in

Stony Creek burned down in 1900, along with the village library and Gilley's store and house. When Stony Creek locals sought to raise funds to build the present Stony Creek Congregational Church building in 1900 and 1901, they circulated an attractive, 20-page brochure around the state. *Stony Creek's Plea,* complete with several photographs, listed the particular needs of three groups of Creekers: quarry workers, islanders, and natives. The pamphlet reflected how these three distinct classes of people in Stony Creek were regarded at the turn of the century. Of the quarry workers, it was said:

The Quarries . . . [in] cutting our beautiful red granite, employ a large number of foreigners—English, Italians, Swedes, Finns, etc. All the educational and religious impulse that most of these people receive must come from the "Church of Christ." We must have an edifice where they can be gathered for social, intellectual, and moral improvement. *This is foreign missionary work and the call is as urgent as any that comes from Darkest Africa, or conservative China.*

The wealthy, prominent islanders, on the other hand, seem to have been revered and certainly not deemed as needy of improvement or missionary outreach. Essentially summer residents, they had more in common culturally and religiously with the Yankee natives. Approached respectfully, and their taxes welcomed, they were nevertheless embraced as outsiders:

"The Thimbles," a group of rocky isles of charming picturesqueness affording the most beautiful scenery on Long Island Sound, attract a large number of resorters every summer. These people coming from large, well-to-do city churches are not easily attracted to a small unpretentious edifice. In order that we may successfully invite our guests to the ministries of Christian worship we need a building that is neat, modern and churchly in appearance.

Despite their middle-class, typically Protestant pride in work, self-sufficiency, and perseverance, the Yankee natives asked for help from others, perhaps with twinges of self-pity:

Stony Creek has a considerable native population. Our boys and girls grow up and go to help make the city. The burden of supporting the church principally rests upon the few who remain. None of our people are wealthy, all have to work for their daily bread, yet with heroic self sacrifice and uncomplaining perseverance we have brought the church to self support. And we will do more! yes, will do our utmost, but it is absolutely impossible for us unaided to provide the building needed to carry on the work demanded. The bulk of the funds must come from abroad. An appeal is made to all our friends to assist.

The pamphlet listed an array of proposed uses for the new building: morning and evening worship, mothers' meetings, youth work, Ladies Aid, community gatherings, weekly services in Swedish, "special lectures and concerts of a high order, given by friends from Yale, the admission price of which is to be within the reach of all," and "monthly meetings of the W.C.T.U." So well known was the Women's Christian Temperance Union that only initials were used.

This viewpoint of the church's mission reflected the challenges created by an evolving population. The descendants of the much earlier European settlers had never seen a time of such protracted change and growth. While their missionary zeal may have been motivated by genuine altruism, it may also have gained energy from a thinly veiled anxiety about differences they neither understood nor especially welcomed.

Immigration and anti-Catholicism in the quarry era

Around 35 million Europeans left the continent between 1840 and 1920. Twelve million people came to the United States between 1890 and 1910 alone. The entire population of the United States in 1890 numbered only around 76 million.

The first great waves of immigrants were of Germans in the 1830s and 1840s and Irish in the 1840s and 1850s. In the 10 years following the Irish Potato Famine of 1845, two and a half million Irish arrived in American ports. By the Civil War in 1860, five million immigrants had come, adding to a native population of only 26 million. Most of these German and Irish immigrants arrived as poor, uneducated Roman Catholics. Large numbers of Chinese also had arrived in the early part of the century, settling primarily in the West. Swedes and Scots came in sizable numbers in the 1870s to Minnesota and the Middle West.

The second massive wave of immigrants included almost three million Italians between 1890 and 1910. Just in the 25 years between 1899 and 1924, there came 3.8 million Italians, 1.8 million Eastern European and Russian Jews, 1.5 million Poles, and 1.3 million Germans, as well as large numbers of Finns, Croats, Slavs, Hungarians, and Ukrainians. Meanwhile, the Western European and Asian immigrants continued to arrive in lesser, although appreciable, numbers.

Such an onslaught of immigrants, the vast majority of whom were Roman Catholic, exposed deeply rooted prejudices and ignorance. Protestant nativism, with its blatant anti-Catholic and anti-foreign rhetoric, arose early and recurred with each new wave of immigration. As early as 1834, prominent Congregational minister Lyman Beecher (1775–1863) railed against Catholics:

If they could read the Bible . . . their darkened intellect would brighten and their bowed mind would rise. If they dared to think for themselves, the contrast of protestant independence with their thral[l]dom, would . . . put an end to an arbitrary clerical domination over trembling superstitious minds.

In Stony Creek, as in other small towns, all foreigners were more quickly assimilated than in the cities. Second and third generations mingled freely and without blatant hostility. In villages, people come to know one another as individuals. They also intermarry. The volunteer fire company, quarrymen's union, public schools, shared military service, factory work in Branford, quarry band, drum corps, lack of ethnic clubs, and small-town life in general served to foster understanding and break down walls of prejudice. *Stony Criker,* a newsletter prepared for men in the military service during World War II in 1943–1944, probably by Rollin Paine, took pains to give equal treatment to both churches.

Although intermarriage was deplored officially by both Catholic and Protestant churches, it had the effect of breaking down distrust. It was common for one spouse to convert to the other's faith, reluctantly and often to the dismay of wider families, while quietly keeping his or her own religious identity. Because the children of such matches were generally reared in one or the other faith, tolerance was fostered even further.

Average, everyday people broke down prejudice long before the churches even tried. Not until after 1977 did Catholics and Congregationalists in Stony Creek begin cooperating with one another. They held occasional joint worship services, shared youth work, sponsored Vacation Bible School programs, rented church facilities, shared in funerals and weddings, and joined other ecumenical efforts in the area. In 1982, it was said: "Stony Creek, Connecticut: There are two churches, one Roman, one Congregational, both Christian. Long ago the Puritans tried to purify the Church of Rome. Today both churches pray and sing together."

These immigrants came for freedom, economic opportunity, and a better life for themselves and their children. They did not come to propagate a popish conspiracy, to destroy the American republican experiment, or to spread anarchism by introducing moral rot within. Alongside desperate need existed idealism. Many believed the inscription on the Statue of Liberty, a poem by Emma Lazarus, though they lacked the skills to read it:

Give me your tired, your poor,
Your huddled masses yearning to breathe free,
The wretched refuse of your teeming shore.
Send these, the homeless, tempest-tost, to me,
I lift my lamp beside the golden door!

—WJ

Main Street looking toward beach

THE GROWTH OF A VILLAGE

The original Yankee settlers in Stony Creek, who came as early as 1671, were farmers and later shipowners. Islands were allotted to settlers as early as 1716, but used mainly for agriculture and fishing. Native Americans from inland still migrated to the shore and islands in the warm summer months at this time, leaving large deposits of oyster shells from their harvests in Stony Creek and along the shoreline.

Before 1852, when the railroad opened, Stony Creek's population was scant. Hotels, islands, and the oyster fishing industry developed rapidly after the opening of the railroad in 1852, drawing large numbers of entrepreneurs from elsewhere in Connecticut and Massachusetts who hoped to take advantage of economic opportunities. The first sizable immigration to Stony Creek, composed primarily of Yankees, occurred in the 1860s and 1870s. The 1880 census lists 21 farmers; 30 boatsmen, fishermen, and oystermen; 27 tradesmen and servants; 20 storekeepers and hotel owners; and 2 professionals. Only five quarrymen are listed. By 1900, the list of quarry workers had grown to 124, not including the several general laborers and blacksmiths who also worked for the quarries.

The 1880 census records only 305 residents in Stony Creek. Of those 305 residents, 242 were born in Connecticut and 38 born elsewhere in the United States. There were 72 year-round residences, 43 summer homes onshore, and 35 on the islands. Those born in England numbered 11, Ireland 6, Sweden 4, Canada 2, and Scotland 1. No Italians are listed. By 1900, the directory lists at least 37 Italians. In 1887, Stony Creek claimed a population of approximately 330. By 1900, that number increased to 1,395 residents.

The actual number of foreign-born, nonresident immigrants who came to Stony Creek is difficult to establish. The great majority of them came because of the quarries. A good estimate suggests that approximately 1,800 were connected with the quarrying between 1887 and 1910. Because quarry workers were much like migrant workers, they moved to available work—typically to the large quarrying centers in Vermont, Rhode Island, Massachusetts, and the Penobscott Bay area in Maine. Sometimes a worker's family stayed in the Stony Creek region while the father traveled afar to work. Sometimes entire families eventually resettled elsewhere.

Beattie's Quarries opened in 1870 in Leete's Island in Guilford; the quarry at Sachem's Head opened in 1871, and the Redpath (later Red Hill) Quarry in 1874. After the Norcross Quarry opened in 1882, the Stony Creek population

57

exploded. At its height in the 1890s, Norcross employed between 600 and 700; Red Hill 100 to 150; Beattie 600 to 700; and Sachem's Head and Brooklyn between 150 and 200. A newspaper account in 1892 mentions a thousand from Red Hill Quarry on strike, but this may in fact refer to all the strikers in the area.

Houses were built so quickly that local historian Gertrude McKenzie later characterized the Stony Creek of that period as a "Western mining boom town." Many new side streets were laid out, and the village grew large enough to open its own Stony Creek Cemetery some time between 1866 and 1872. Union Chapel was built in 1866 and enlarged in 1877 because of the growing population. The Stony Creek Congregational Church was gathered in 1874. A parsonage was built in 1892 and 1893. The church conducted two Sunday services and had a Sunday school enrollment of 170 in 1898. The Sons of St. George built their hall in 1891, the same year the guild was founded in Stony Creek, at what is now 20 School Street. The International Order of Odd Fellows, established in the Creek in 1892, purchased Seaside Hall—formerly Frink's Roller Skating Rink and today the home of the Stony Creek Fife and Drum Corps.

Fraternal orders such as the Sons of St. George, Odd Fellows, and Pythians were all

English or American. The sons of St. George was an order of English quarry workers. The quarrymen's union generally met in St. George's Hall on School Street, as did entertainers, traveling troupes, and political groups. Odd Fellows used Seaside Hall as their meeting place, with a busy program of activities, as well as public dances and entertainments. The secret, male fraternal orders often offered death and disability benefits, besides active social, benevolent, and community programs, and served in their earlier days as precursors to trade unions.

Both census and school population figures paint a picture of rapid expansion. The "little red schoolhouse," the area's first, was located at Spitzer's Rock near 550 Leete's Island Road and used from 1788 to 1865. It grew from the 20 students of 1864 to 120 by 1877. A second school building was erected in 1865 at the present Reilly house at 44 School Street, with another building soon constructed next to it in the present Land Trust Building at 26 School Street. In the same period, another schoolhouse was built at Hoadley's Neck in Guilford, before that area seceded and became a part of Guilford in 1885. Records show that the school population grew so dramatically that in 1892, money was appropriated to build a new, three-story, frame

The school building at
28 School Street

school building at 28 School Street. By 1900, the new school was conducting double sessions. The Branford Town Report for 1890 noted that the Stony Creek School was crowded "on account of the constant accession of families as fast as houses are provided for them," and that "it was necessary, because of lack of room, to refuse admission to quite a number." Even as late as 1910, private residences were used to accommodate classroom overflow. The building at 28 School Street remained in operation until 1981, when it was closed and converted into offices for several small businesses.

The Norcross Quarry built 15 to 20 small houses on quarry land for workers and their families. The buildings are all gone now, but some foundation holes can still be seen on the hill south of the quarry proper. Beattie's Quarries erected its own village that included the Beattie family home, a boardinghouse, at least 20 small houses, a grocery and dry goods store, and a hall where Catholic masses were celebrated regularly by priests from Guilford.

In the boom years of the 1890s, many Stony Creek hotels rented rooms to quarry workers,

especially in the off-season months. It was common also for Stony Creek natives to rent rooms to quarry workers. It is said that just about every household rented rooms during the boom period. Colorful stories survive of single stonecutters renting rooms, removing furniture, and bringing in mattresses to save money so they could "really live it up over the weekends."

In addition to quarry-owned housing at Norcross, two sizable boardinghouses consistently filled up with workers. The Lazzari/Bardi/DaRos Boarding House was the largest. The three-story, 150-foot (45.7-meter) building had 45 unheated bedrooms, a common dining hall, two smoking rooms, and living quarters for the proprietors. Angelina DaRos was responsible for providing 60 workers with three hot meals a day, doing their laundry, cleaning the rooms, and even emptying the commodes—all without running water. The structure survived until 1959, when it was torn down and replaced with a new small house.

The Gilley Boarding House, west of the quarry, was smaller. It is sometimes reported that English and Americans typically stayed at Gilley's, while Italians, Swedes, and Finns stayed at the DaRos Boarding House. Owen Berio writes in his history of the quarries: "It was an unofficial rule, which was neither confirmed nor

59

ordered, that all foreigners had to board at the company boardinghouse if single; if they didn't they soon lost their job."

Local residents continue to debate the question of ethnic separation, whether forced, voluntary, or existent at all. Some insist that no ethnic separation ever took place, and that may be the case, especially after 1910. But in the quarrying heyday of the 1890s, the English quite naturally gravitated to Gilley's for social and cultural comfort, while Italians, Swedes, and Finns boarded at DaRos's for similar reasons. No evidence exists of a "forced" housing arrangement. Peter DaRos Sr., recalls Germans, Spanish, Irish, Portuguese, Swedes, Italians, English, and others all boarding in the same house at the same time.

THE DAROS
BOARDING HOUSE
With its 63 rooms, the boardinghouse could accommodate up to 50 boarders plus the family that ran it. In addition to the bedrooms, the building included dining rooms, smoking rooms, and a big kitchen. There was no central heat or running water.

60

Because of prejudice against early Swedish arrivals in the quarries, they may have had to retreat to Goat Island at night after work. Swedes are said to have kept herds of goats for milk on this island, now known as Bear Island.

The number of immigrants who settled in Stony Creek was never large enough to sustain the ethnic institutions common in the cities and larger quarrying centers. Italians in Barre, Vermont, arrived in sufficient number to establish churches, socialist halls, union halls, athletic clubs, social clubs, and cooperative stores. In Rockport and Lanesville, Massachusetts, Scandinavian Lutherans started churches, and an active temperance society with its own building, bands, theater groups, ethnic stores and cooperatives, and even a socialist hall with a full program of activities. Finns there vehemently divided themselves into church Finns, socialist Finns, and real Communist Finns, each with their own institutions and prejudices.

Stony Creek did have its own Swedish Lutheran Church, organized in 1888. A chapel was built sometime between that year and 1892. The foundation hole is still visible in the woods on Leete's Island Road across from Flat Rock Road Extension. There the congregation held Swedish-language services under the area's first Swedish pastor, Reverend Jacobson. Prior to that, Swedish churchgoers had to wait for occasional Swedish Lutheran services to be conducted at Union Chapel. The Swedish Lutheran Church closed in 1920 and donated its equipment to the Swedish Lutheran Church— now Tabor— in Branford. Its society funds were used for the pipe organ at the Stony Creek Congregational Church. Although the Church was planning to hold weekly services in Swedish as early as 1901, there is no record of this ever actually happening.

A sizable Catholic population resided in Stony Creek and Leete's Island beginning in the 1880s. Sometime in the early 1890s, they approached the region's bishop to form a parish and church in Stony Creek, but were directed to the Leete's Island mission at Beattie's Quarries, where a hall had been built in 1888 for Catholic masses. In later years, a priest offered mass at St. George's Hall. St. Therese Church was built and consecrated in 1927.

About three-quarters of the quarry immigrants who settled in Stony Creek came from the Cornwall area on the southwest coast of England. Many stonecutters left Cornwall— famous for its Celtic culture, mining, and fishing industries—and came to the United States when the stone industry of England declined in the late 1800s.

Cornish families typically associated with the Congregational Church, but many were not entirely satisfied. In 1899, 13 English people withdrew from the Congregational Church to form a Methodist-Episcopal Church in Stony Creek that met at St. George's Hall. Following successful evangelistic services in 1894, weekly class meetings, or small study and discipline groups, were formed, and "the English brethren especially were glad of it, and others approved." "With more encouragement from outside," they formed their own church. Neither deep-rooted dissatisfaction nor doctrinal controversy seemed to explain their decision, but rather ethnic identity, possibly combined with religious revival. Congregational records state: "Many of these, and their children, had been much helped by our church work as a whole . . . but [they had a] preference for the Methodist-Episcopal order, with which they had previously been associated, in England and elsewhere. . . . It is hoped that by the two, still more work will be done for the common cause of Christ in this community." Within five years, in 1904, all but one of the 13 were received back into the Congregational Church. Children of these families became noted for the singing of Cornish Christmas carols and the making of pasties and lemon water.

61

Stony Creek train station

Scots, mostly from the Aberdeen quarrying and fishing region in northeastern Scotland, came to Stony Creek and Leete's Island early. Captain John Beattie was himself of Scottish descent. Seven Scottish families settled in the boom years. The fact that Cornish and Scottish newcomers were generally English-speaking Protestants no doubt aided their rapid assimilation into Yankee culture.

Irish, Swedes, Finns, and Italians were not as quickly assimilated. The Irish immigration to America was the earliest and most resisted. Sixteen Irish families are listed as having settled in Stony Creek as early as 1890, but it took generations for them to establish their place in the community. Prejudice against them lingered longer than against any other group. When fire destroyed the quarry boardinghouse on Granite Island, now known as Rogers Island, locals readily laid the blame at the feet of an Irish domestic servant. "It seems the woman, she is Irish I believe, who kept the house and boarded the men, had gone to New Haven that day," writes a Creeker of that time. "The girls, three or four of them, were all up in the attic and did not know any thing about it until the house was in flames." In 1887, Peter Coffee, an Irish quarry worker, was convicted of the murder of the train station manager, Charlie Way,

who was tied to the train tracks and killed by a train. After a lengthy trial that received detailed coverage in New Haven newspapers, Coffee was given a life sentence—he died two years later in the Wethersfield Prison. Such incidents could only reinforce prejudices against the Irish.

Sixteen Swedish families settled in Stony Creek's boom years. No Finns are listed in this period, although they were working the quarries in 1900. Others settled after the turn of the century. To the Yankee natives, the Swedes and Finns often seemed indistinguishable. However, the immigrants themselves certainly knew the difference—there were true Swedes, Swedish-speaking Finns from southern Finland, and Finnish-speaking Finns from northern Finland— and they carried ancient ethnic rivalries to their new home that stemmed from centuries of Swedish conquest in the Old World.

Seven Italian families are connected with early quarrying. Although some were present in the 1890s, many more Italians came to work the quarries after the turn of the century. Records from Stony Creek Cemetery list "2 Italian babies" buried there, but fail to include their names, parents' names, birth or death dates, or even gravestones.

In other quarry locations, Italians sometimes

Linden Point

received treatment as harsh as that leveled at the Irish. At both Barre, Vermont, and Cape Ann, Massachusetts, Italians were enlisted as strike breakers without their knowledge. Just "off the boat," looking for work—not knowing a word of English—and herded off by their "padrones," the Italian "scabs" were shot, stoned, and in a few cases killed when they got to the quarries. No reports exist of such abuse in Stony Creek.

Robert Beattie, son of the Beattie's Quarries owner, believed that many of the Italians came to the United States "because they had a price on their heads—in trouble with the courts. A lot of these guys were bad news and came from the Trieste area of Italy." So violent could life be at the Sachem's Head Quarry that Frank Paviglionite took a pearl-handled pistol to bed with him "because even your best friend would rob you." Narcissa Tonelli and her husband came to Sachem's Head in 1908. Of Henry Ponti, a relative and informal recruiter, she said: "Mr. Ponti scoured the streets of New York for prospects. One time he brought a railroad car full of tramps out of the Bowery."

Summer cottagers were quick to commend Italian workers over native Creekers when controversy arose over the Red Hill Quarry opening at Flying Point in 1890:

The residents and the cottagers are unanimous in their praise of the conduct of the laborers, which are for the most part Italians. These laborers are quiet, inoffensive, and industrious and cause no trouble whatever. They board at different places and have never set foot on the hotel steps, as has been reported. In fact, cottagers esteem more highly these same Italians than they do some of the natives of Stony Creek.

Part of what won praise for the Italian workers was the fact that they "never set foot on the hotel steps" and were out of public view up in the woods.

The quarry industry itself involved two tiers of people: supervisors and workers. Owners and supervisors generally came from the ranks of middle-class Protestants. Workers were largely itinerant, single, lower class, and uneducated. In the quarrying heyday between 1890 and 1910, many workers were immigrant, Catholic, and poor. Workers, at least in the early years, stayed within their social enclaves, traveling to whatever quarrying centers had work available. The prominent cottagers were remarkably complimentary, if condescending, toward the quarry workers. Their disdain was directed at the Stony Creek natives.

63

EDGEWATER COURT
The Victorian cottages on
Long Point, which were
later destroyed by the
hurricane of 1938.

AN UNEASY COEXISTENCE

As it turned out, quarry workers tended in some
cases to be isolated. In her history of the region,
Linda Trowbridge Baxter notes:

The residents of Guilford center had very little contact
with the quarries. Quarrymen lived on the site, in Leete's
Island or in Stony Creek but virtually none settled in the
Borough of Guilford. Provisions, both food and
clothing, which were not purchased at the Leete's Island
general store owned by the Beatties or in Stony Creek
were brought in by local Guilford businessmen. It has
been suggested that this arrangement was by design to

keep the quarry workers at a distance from the town, but
this assertion would be difficult to prove.

Quarries on the water, ideal for shipping, did not
always mix well with summer vacation cottages.
What was true in Guilford was true in Stony
Creek, as well—perhaps more so, although for
different reasons. Baxter writes:

[I]n Sachem's Head, "quarrying irked the summer
cottagers across the harbor to no end." Blasting
caused constant dust and noise. Spillage from the
mining washed into the Sound and polluted the bathers'
water and bothered lobstermen. Residents even

requested that the locomotive whistle, "which resembled the screech of a mockingbird," be replaced with a more pleasant sound.

A controversy that arose in 1892 over quarrying offers a fascinating glimpse into the sometimes uneasy coexistence within the three-tiered Stony Creek class structure. In 1890, the Red Hill Quarry bought the Island View House, a hotel on Stony Creek's Flying Point. When the quarry managers proceeded to set up quarrying operations smack in the midst of an area of fine, new, expensive homes, "they did it under a vigorous protest from the many cottagers at Flying Point and Camp's Hill [Prospect Hill]." A lengthy newspaper article reported:

Certain reports concerning the rapid degeneration of Stony Creek as a summer resort have been circulating recently, that were without foundation. . . . The introduction of this quarry business is the cause of all the reports as to the degeneration of Stony Creek and it must be admitted that it does bring in an element which cannot be said to be truly consistent with a popular summer resort.

There may have been worry that quarry workers would be housed in the hotel rooms, although no

RAND POINT (COE'S DOCK ON LONG POINT ROAD), STONY CREEK
Questions exist about how this dock was used. Here flatcars carry granite to be loaded onto the waiting boats. Local memories suggest that the dock was also used to bring coal into Stony Creek.

Island View House,
also known as Flying
Point Hotel

indication exists that this occurred. Apparently, the hotel continued operation with summer tourists boarding, even though it was "within hearing distance of the stonecutters' hammer. . . . [I]t is far from being a noisy and turbulent place. The place is very neatly kept and the guests . . . are among the best."

Good reports to the contrary, tension continued among the three groups: cottagers, natives, and quarry owners. Cottagers were prominent, wealthy, cultured, civic-minded, professional businessmen. They were generally summer boarders who lived at water's edge ("downstreet"), as well as islanders. Largely English and Protestant, they built their Victorian "cottages" along the shoreline. Senator William J. Clark built the crown jewel of the summer homes atop Prospect Hill in 1880—a classic Victorian stick cottage with a 60-foot (18.3-meter) tower, designed by Henry Austin (1804–1891). The

General Pargoud cottage and Lewis-Fisher cottage were built in the same period.

Cottagers readily voiced their perspective about property values and status. Local historian John Kirby compiled a sampling of their views: "Stony Creek is still frequented by many prominent people." "There are now on the hill 14 fine cottages, and they are kept in the finest of shape." "The lawns are beautifully kept and the private road up the hill is one of the finest shell roads in the country." "The Camp Hill residents have invested there $75,000 in their places, while the Granite company may have invested $10,000 in their places at the foot of the hill, and the cottagers very righteously ask, 'Are we, the larger, to be driven away by the smaller?'"

As successful, prominent businessmen, cottagers cited the impracticality of transporting the granite 2 miles (3.2 km) from the quarry to the Point and then 2 miles back to the railroad links. They also criticized the quarry owners for their bad business sense in locating in the cottagers' midst.

Stony Creek natives took their stand on the side of the quarries. Stony Creek shopkeepers and tradesmen benefited far more from the large number of quarry workers and their families than they did from the wealthy summer residents and the hotels. The Red Hill Quarry, according to newspaper records, employed "about 1,000 hands and had a weekly pay roll of about $10,000. This, of course, was very advantageous to the business of the town," but was detrimental to the resort trade.

Antagonism arose between cottagers and natives Creekers, as well, over the formation of "a progressive and efficient village improvement society," one of the predecessors of the present-day Stony Creek Association. The Village Improvement Society developed primarily through the efforts of the summer cottagers. With a good deal of labor, they cut brush and filled swampland. They raised and installed sidewalks, railings, and 45 gas streetlights. Of $1,250 in contributions, only $100 came from natives, and only a few at that. Again John Kirby's compilation allows us to listen in:

The 'natives,' so the cottagers say, not only took no interest, but lent all sorts of resistance to their efforts. . . . After the lampposts had been placed by the society the citizens were not willing to light them at a cost of one cent a day. From this can be seen the struggle which the cottagers have to make in carrying on their improvements.

The view of Camp's Hill (Prospect Hill) from the Red Hill Quarry property

Natives, by and large, had come to Stony Creek to serve the hotels, build new houses, and work the oyster beds. Middle-class tradesmen, storekeepers, and small-scale entrepreneurs came to take advantage of economic opportunities as Stony Creek developed into a summer resort. Although the first hotel was built in 1846 on Pot Island, six other hotels flourished between 1860 and 1920—and some as long afterward as the 1950s. The economic benefit was appreciable, as Linda Trowbridge Baxter details. "Those who think the large quarries are of no financial benefit to the town," she quotes a local of the time as saying, "should see the loads of meat and provisions that J.E. Norton and Son carry down there every day. Nearly a ton of beef is consumed every week, together with a load of vegetables." Baxter continues:

More than just increasing the tax base . . . the quarries provided increased trade for local business. . . . Benton's Market made regular rounds with groceries and dry goods to the quarries. Mr. Julian of Whitfield Street became a vegetable vendor to the quarries of both Guilford and Stony Creek. Mrs. Ryerson recalled that with the regular delivery of meat, milk and dry goods, it was possible for her mother almost never to leave her home.

The cottagers on Camp's Hill included seven businessmen, three politicians, one military general, and one clergyman. These men appear to have been sensitive to charges that the poor were oppressed. J.H. Bartholomew, a manufacturer and president of the New Haven and Derby Railroad, died at his cottage in 1884. His obituary noted that:

Religiously he was a Congregationalist . . . though of late he has not been a member of it, differences of opinion having caused him to withdraw. He, however . . . always kept close to the cross, and by the uprightness of his walk and purity of his life ennobled the cause of his Master. . . . Mr. Bartholomew began life as a poor man. By industry and economy he died possessed of ample fortune. . . . He can in no sense be regarded as the oppressor of the poor, but rather the friend and encourager of the struggling.

Not merely sensitive to public perceptions and national labor trends, these shrewd, successful businessmen surely watched the national labor movement with close attention—and they made their own accommodations to the rising tide of discontent.

—WJ

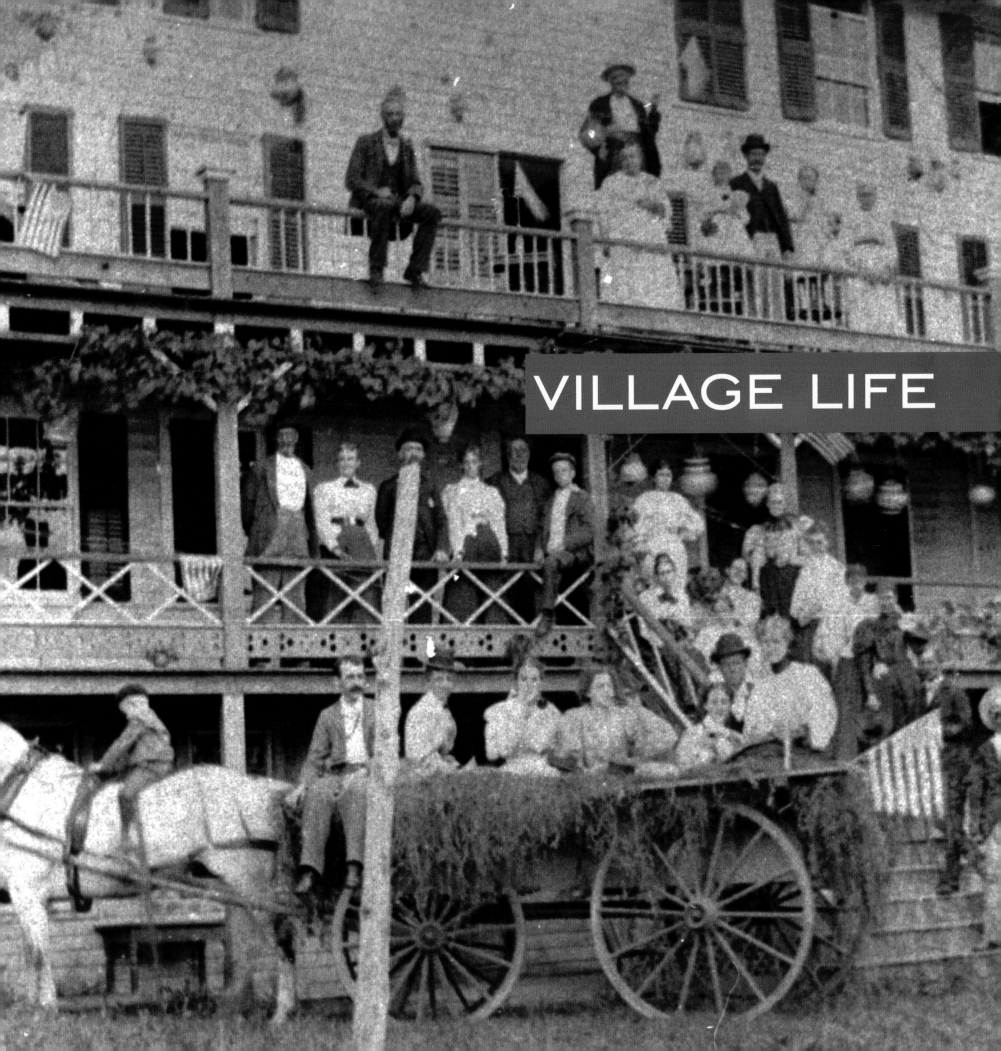

VILLAGE LIFE

Ponder the Stony Creek of 100 years ago.

Oxen. Tubas. Coal ciphers. Ice wagons. Over-packed trunks. Clanking trolleys. Smoky trains. Noisy saloons. Gas lamps. Photographs from that time show stony eyes, stern faces, and hard-working hands. Yet these were people of flesh and bone, not so different from people today. They, too, hoped for a meaningful life, longed for love and laughter, and believed in a good future for their children.

Still, consider. They had no cars, no paved roads, but rather bumped along in horse-drawn carriages or climbed the high steps of trundling trains and trolleys. The air around them smelled of smoke, horses, rotting fish, and tidal water. They had no indoor plumbing, and winter carried a particular bite when the time came to visit the outhouse. They had no refrigerators, so summer meant calling for the ice wagon, burying the ice blocks in sawdust, and letting chips melt in their mouths.

They had no firetrucks or ambulances. When a fiery tragedy struck, they pulled that pumper with bare hands or raced to the fire in a bucket brigade. The village doctor made calls. And a reputed elixir could be had for a price from the traveling Kickapoo Indians. But there was no elixir when the quarrymen coughed blood and gurgled with silicosis caused by stone dust. And quarry accidents happened again and again.

Electricity was rare. So were telephones. A knock at the door might mean a telegram, and with it anxiety—until the news brought a smile of relief or weeping over tragedy from afar. Forget television, computers, or even radio. Substitute board games, fraternal clubs, marching bands, union meetings, church, books, and of course, work. Creekers might take in a silent movie at the Stony Creek theater. Or they'd laugh to the entertainment at one of the hotels, maybe dance at Seaside Hall, or socialize and unwind at one of the Creek's seven saloons.

Then there were the beaches, islands, and blue waters. No bare chests, though—not even the men. A steam launch, properly stoked, lugged heavy wooden trunks to an island. And maybe residents would indulge in a romantic sail at dusk. The tourists arrived on steamers out of New Haven and on trolleys. Many hotels competed for their commerce. Some establishments had better food, some better oysters, some better entertainment, some better beds, some better service.

There were novelties to be had, as well. Maybe not the girls at the ice cream parlor, but certainly the new-fangled ice cream—and photographs, still young as technologies went. A shopping trip meant meat at one store, vegetables at another, and newspapers at another. Perhaps most novel of all were the accents, the broken English, the strange religions of the newcomers looking for quarry work. And the Creekers would criticize foreign lands on the street; argue politics, religion, and union violence at the barber shop; or gossip at the post office. And they would cut red granite. Construct a church. Grow a village.

—WJ

The *Lucy*

Unidentified woman and child in rowboat

Bathers at the beach

TROLLEY JUNCTION

CIRCA 1910

The trolley line from New Haven met the line to Guilford at the end of the present Thimble Islands Road (then Main Street).

76

Trolley station

Adelaide Lazzari (Nagetti) and Annie Hinkley selling lemonade at the trolley station

The Stony Creek Band antedated the Drum Corps.

Stony Creek Drum Corps

Outside the ice cream shop

Northrop's store, Flying
Point

Frank and Harvey Brainerd with their model ships

Antonio Lazzari, the Constable, on his motor bike

Rose Russell in a rowboat

Ox team in front of the
Edwards' house

Thomas Bray, the village blacksmith, standing beside a three-horse carriage

THE FIRST PUMPER
Standing beside the pumper are John B. Russell and Al Sutherland, who was Superintendent at the Norcross Quarry.

Members of the Stony Creek Fire Department in front of the Stony Creek school

Ball's oyster dock

PROSPECT HILL BEACH

Three of the children are identified as Helen Converse Orr, Agnes Curtiss Church, and Lewis Baldwin Church.

Hooghkirk house

The Indian Point House

Mother Brainerd's house

The town dock

Elton and Wheeler Barnes
atop Brainerd's windmill

VILLAGE FOLK
Attilio Banca (on rocking
horse), Annie Lazzari, two
friends, Daly Lazzari
Magnetti, and Victor
(standing); Anita and
Mary Acebo (in front)

The ice wagon

Far left: Ample provisions for the residents of Stony Creek in one of the local shops

Near left: C.A. Russell's store

Main Street looking north toward Brainerd's

Far left: George Christy sitting outside his first studio

Near left: The tent on the grounds of the present Church of Christ

YOUNG GIRLS CARRYING A BABY'S COFFIN
Identified are Lena Columbo, Annie Lazzari, Daly Lazzari, Marie LaVassa, Caroline Lazzari, Rose Lazzari Cogliati.

LIFE IN THE QUARRIES

QUARRYMEN AT WORK

It was common in the late 1800s for a business that was the major employer in town to provide housing for its employees—usually in a way that reinforced the social hierarchy of the company. Dwellings increased in size and amenities as one moved higher in the organization. Workers moved regularly from quarry to quarry. These factors—combined in Stony Creek with the emerging social distinctions of cottagers, natives, and quarry workers in the community—made the quarry social structure less entrenched than in other industries. Even so, status was often revealed by whether a worker owned a home, boarded in someone else's home, or resorted to the quarry-run boardinghouses.

The Italians, who had a centuries-old heritage of working in stone, dominated the influx into the quarries and tended more than any of the other groups to acquire the more skilled stonecutter jobs. But of necessity, they worked alongside the Germans, Irish, Cornish, Scots, Swedes, Finns, Spanish, and Portuguese who arrived, as well.

This ethnic diversity seems to have cast more color on the social life at work and in community in Stony Creek than the company hierarchy. Reports vary as to the extent of the segregation and animosity among these ethnic groups and whether the quarry owners tried to use the animus to keep the workers from organizing into effective unions. But it is clear that a worker's ethnicity was the first factor that distinguished him.

The industrialization of quarry work meant that each quarry function required a certain kind of worker, and the worker's job title defined both the work and the man. The union charter of 1891 gives a list of jobs that includes laborers, derrickmen, head derrickmen, blacksmith helpers, blacksmiths, steam drillers, powdermen, engineers, stone breakers, stonecutters, master mechanics, powerhouse engineers, boxers, and loaders. Pay scales in contracts evidence the pecking order—ranging from 21 to 35 cents an hour.

Thirty cents an hour for six 10-hour days

Quarry workers standing
outside a shed

93

Doc Townsend

doing such backbreaking work strikes us today as exploitative—and perhaps it was. But working six long days was common then, and the price of goods seems to us today astoundingly cheap. A gallon of milk in 1890 sold for about a nickel, and a house could be built for under 1,000 dollars. Furthermore, workers incurred no significant commuting costs. Workers who lived in town walked to work unless they were far enough down the street to use the trolleys that came into use in about 1905.

Apparently, quarry workers didn't find quarry work to be any worse than other work that was available. As Eleanor Leighton observes:

When the quarries weren't working in the winter, many [workers] would apply to work at the Malleable Iron Fittings Company, Wire Company, or Branford Lock Works in Branford Center. They were called "snowbirds" and often turned away because as soon as the quarries opened up they would return to work in them.

Accidents were a frequent fact of life in the quarries as bone battled stone with the double-edged power of machinery. When the steam whistle blasted three times to signal the doctor, families would rush, panic-stricken from their homes to see what had happened.

Doc Townsend and Doc McQueen often treated mangled fingers and crushed toes. Town records detail drownings, skull fractures, black powder explosions, falling derricks, and train track accidents. Carl Balestracci, whose family roots extend into the quarries, recounts how in 1914, his uncle was working on the face of a ledge when another worker brought a derrick around and didn't see him. He was knocked down and the stone fell on him.

One accident, a well-remembered account from *The Shoreline Times,* provides a graphic description of the dangers of quarry work. In May 1870, while a sloop was being loaded with stone for the Brooklyn Bridge, "the stop holding the gaff broke, letting it fall to the ground crushing a worker to a pulp."

When the stone for the Battle Monument at West Point was being cut, the 41-foot (12.5-meter) long stone shaft shifted and crushed a worker's foot and ankle. In 1914, a worker was killed in Beattie's Quarries when a boulder fell and hit him. In 1922, at Norcross Quarry, a man on a ladder oiling the top of a polishing machine was pushed off by a moving crane, fell, struck his head, and died. When the boiler operator at Norcross tried filling the hot boiler with cold water, it blew up and killed him. Eleanor Leighton records:

This nimble "grease monkey" (Alex Greenvall) may be climbing to the top of the derrick either to grease the pulley or to apply a coat of creosote to help preserve the wooden pole.

The boiler actually went through the roof, hit the ledge above, and seemed to hover for a moment, giving the men working below time to get out of the way.

There's no doubt that quarry work took grit and guts, whether it was drilling, blasting, cutting stone—or climbing to the top of a tall derrick to grease its fittings, as did a derrickman nicknamed "Grease Monkey Ricciotti." As Stony Creek's Wayne Jacobson notes:

'Grease Monkey Ricciotti' normally maintained the 100-foot [30.5-meter] derrick at the Red Hill Quarry. The derrick was set on the top of the ledge, with the quarry hole down at least another 50 feet [15.25 m]— over 150 feet [45.7 m] in all. Ricciotti thought nothing of going to the top. Sometimes he placed himself at the end of the derrick's arm, and workers swung him around as he was lifted up to the top.

One time Ricciotti was sick, and the wheel at the top needed fixing. Old Bernard Page volunteered to go up. He climbed the spikes on the derrick about 50 feet into the air. Page made the mistake of looking down. He panicked—looking down at the water and stones a hundred feet below. And he froze! Page never did make it to the top. And could never figure out how he got down. For '[C]razy Ricciotti' it was nothing. . . .

Quarry worker jobs

blacksmith	did all the iron fabricating, which mostly involved forging and sharpening tools
carpenter	built wooden boxes or frames for shipping the granite
derrickman	maintained the derricks, including climbing the structure to grease the fittings
engineer	worked the hoisting engines on the derricks and ran the steam boilers in the powerhouse and the locomotives
powderman	was responsible for handling the black powder used for excavation
quarryman	unskilled laborer whose job was to cut stone from ledge
stonecutter	skilled worker who did the finish cutting and carving of stone based on a diagram; often the best carvers were Italians
tool boy or tool carrier	shuttled tools that required sharpening between workers and blacksmiths; had a wire basket for toting tools; one tool boy for each blacksmith

Whether it was the ruggedness of the work or the environment created by an all-male work scene, the men could be as hard on each other as the granite and machinery were on them. Newcomers had to prove their worth, and initiates, such as tool boys, had to go through their share of hazing. Leonard Page says of his experience as a tool boy:

I worked in the quarry when I was 14 or 15 years old, carrying water and as a tool boy. I used to go to the blacksmith shop and put a dozen or so of the plug drills—a foot [0.3 m] or so long and about an inch [2.54 cm] in diameter—in what you call a shot bag. Then I'd go and climb the ladders to get where the stonecutters were working.

Sometimes I'd get up to just the top level, and some old stonecutter would want to have some fun. He'd take his foot and kick my face full of stone dust. It'd take me a while to get that out of my eyes.

Then, of course, we'd carry a piece of waste cloth in our pocket for wiping our hands off of the grease and stuff. You'd be walking along, and the first thing you'd know, you'd see flames going up your back. Somebody had touched a match to it.

When you were a tool boy, you got your head dunked in the cooling barrel used by the blacksmiths. And at some point you had to get up on a block of stone and take your little fellow out and show

how you were hung. Sometimes you got a little grease on it.

It took about a year or more before they caught me. I kept away from them for a long time. Like, one day I went down at noon to the carpenter shop. This big fellow, 'Johnny Apple,' got a hold of the back of my belt, and he said, 'I guess we got you this time, Pagie.' I made one jolt, and the belt broke, so they didn't get me that time.

Then Johnny Wilson, the blacksmith, sent me to ask Stan Barnes to send up a man. Not thinking about it, I headed down to the sheds. I went in this door, and somebody stood in front of me and to each side, so I had to throw up my hands and go through my treatment."

Replete with their own perils, stone and machinery in combination introduced an altogether new threat to the health of the quarry worker—silicosis, the stonecutter's own form of black lung disease. Using machinery to cut and carve the stone produced great clouds of stone dust. The atmosphere inside the cutting sheds is said to have been a perpetual London fog.

Masks, nose clips, or pads were available to catch the dust and provide protection, but typically, the only time the men would wear them was when the representative of the insurance company came by for inspection. Doc Townsend is reported to have said that those who used

INTERIOR OF A WORK SHED
The bridge crane that appears overhead was used for moving heavy pieces of stone into place.

STEAM ENGINE
The steam engine, also
called a hoisting engine,
powered the derricks.

chewing tobacco lived longer because the
tobacco would catch some of the stone and steel
dust. The men believed that growing big, bushy
mustaches helped keep the dust out of nostrils
and mouths, and some drank whiskey to relieve a
coughing jag.

Quarryman Aldo Balestracci said of silicosis,
"Everyone knew about it, but what of it? It
was a way of life." The folklore was that in the
three years it took to become a journeyman
stonecutter, you already would have developed
a case of silicosis. Locals claimed that when
workers started coughing blood, they started
carving their own gravestones. If so, the ailing
workers must have been buried elsewhere,
since very few of the memorials in the Stony
Creek Cemetery are fabricated from Stony Creek
pink granite.

Eventually, as the illness developed, a sick
man's lungs would hemorrhage. The second
hemorrhage usually resulted in death. The
dust actually constituted a danger to the whole
neighborhood, because it could spread over a
large area.

Captain John Beattie, the owner of Beattie's
Quarries, always insisted that his workers work
outside, even in winter. He claimed that his
approach virtually eliminated the killer disease
from his quarry—especially in comparison to

other quarries in the area. No doubt it helped, but the town's statistics indicate that a fair number of stonecutters at Beattie's Quarries died of lung disease nevertheless.

The industrialization of quarry work also introduced labor unions. In September of 1890, the workers of Stony Creek joined the Quarrymen's National Union of the United States of America, and in 1892, the workers went on strike for the first time. That strike and a later one in 1897—both predicated on wage disputes—were fairly brief and resolved without causing much harm to the quarry business. But the lockout in March of 1900 took longer to resolve and brought the quarries to the abrupt end of their boom years. Liza Carroll writes:

In 1900, the stonecutters asked for 33¢ an hour and an 8-hour day. The company wouldn't agree to the increase, so the men went out on strike on March 1, 1900. On March 31, Norcross and the stonecutters agreed on 33¢ and 34¢ an hour for an eight hour day, but a Mr. Duncan, secretary of the National Stonecutters Union told the men to quit work or surrender their charter. By April 21 the men decided to stop work. There was subsequently a second settlement in May 1900 for a penny more an hour, a 14% increase in the piece bill, and the contract was to run for 3 years.

Quarry workers at the derrick

The national economic depression that began in 1887 created that all too familiar business predicament of having to reduce the price of the product while responding to workers who wanted to see their incomes continue to grow. By 1900, the rising availability of concrete and steel was putting tremendous price pressure on granite.

—RD

99

The human cost of the quarries

It was common knowledge that a life spent working in the quarries was going to be a shortened one, whether by accident, injury, or quarry worker's disease—

This observation characterizes the memories and writings of many people involved with or interested in the quarries. When you chose to be a quarry worker—quarryman, stonecutter, polisher, carver, railroad worker, bargeman, mechanic, carpenter, blacksmith, or laborer—your life was on the line, and the odds were against you.

One survivor of the quarries' heyday, Leonard Page, still recalls the accidents:

The freight yard . . . had a metal derrick. It had a boom on it, and there they had these gears . . . and a drum with a wire that two men turned the crank on to raise the stones up. One day, a man named Jerry Lucarelli was lifting a stone. The door didn't catch just right, so he took a railroad spike and put it in the gear. When he let go, the gear broke all to pieces. One piece went right through his stomach and the other piece went way up on Bowhay Hill, and pieces were found way down by the railroad bridge to the west. You had to get [the gear] in a certain place before the door would drop into the teeth to hold it. It wasn't quite there so [Jerry] stuck the railroad spike in. And that was too bad for him because it killed him dead as a maggot!

The quarrying part of it was dangerous. You never knew when you were going to get caught in a stone. . . . One [worker] got his head caught between a couple of stones and smashed his ears in pretty good. . . . He was a little Italian fellow, full of the devil, and jumping around like a bullfrog all the time, anyway, but he got his head caught between the stones. . . . [T]he stone cutters would get a piece of steel [in them]. I'd have to take them to the doctor's somewhere. As I say, I've taken as many as three a day.

Ben DeNardi, 74 at the time of this interview, worked in the quarries, as well. He recounts his own near tragedies related to the work:

Early in the morning it was cold. Of course, everything froze. If it rained, it froze. It was slippery with ice. The big hooks that they had [would] snap, it would be so cold. We used to heat them in big barrels. . . .

There was a little walkway halfway up the ledge we would walk across to get down to the other spot. One day there was ice on one spot and a little bit of snow had come down. All of a sudden, [I slipped]. . . . What saved me was a guard. That was a scary day!

Another day, on that same walkway, I was walking there and putting a big stone down the hole. They had a small chain [there and] I knew that the chain was too small for that stone. I'm up in the spot there [and] the chain snaps! The hook landed way up in the woods. A piece of chain went right behind my head. I could see it coming at me—where I was going to go! That was close. They found the hook [a quarter] mile away at the Boy Scout camp.

John Barnes, who was quarry superintendent for 31 years and an absolute stickler for safety, observed that every time you set off explosives in the quarry ". . . it was an experiment! You never could predict the outcome exactly." In one way or another, the quarry workers faced the possibility that they would not return home at the end of the day's work.

Local historian Joel Helander reviewed Guilford town records from between 1876 and 1918 and found the deaths of 34 quarry workers recorded for that period. Eleven of the men were born in Ireland, six in Finland, four in Sweden, four in the United States, two in Italy, one in Hungary, and one in Scotland (three had no birthplace recorded). Of those 34 men, six died of lung disease (almost certainly related to quarrying). Another 17 died accidental deaths: "railroad accident," "blown up in a blast," "fractured skull," "drowned," "crushed by a falling derrick." Witnesses said that young workers would sometimes drop simply from exhaustion or dehydration.

Even when no cause of death was recorded or natural causes were cited, it is safe to assume that the hard life of the quarry worker and the heavy drinking at local saloons at work's end had a profound effect on mortality. Of the 34 men referred to above, seven were in their twenties when they died, six were in their thirties, three were in their forties, and eight were in their fifties. Only eight of the 34 made it to age 60 or older.

Perhaps the worst consequence of quarry work was the so-called *quarryman's disease*, silicosis. Silicosis results from the introduction of the mineral silica into the human lung. The concentration of silica dust one inhales, and the length of time it is inhaled, determine the ultimate manifestations of the disease. ➤

The human cost of the quarries *(continued)*

At best, it is a disabling disease. More often, it is implicated in the appearance of other diseases of the lungs. With or without complicating conditions, however, silicosis is often lethal.

Silica is the most common mineral on earth, used in many industrial processes. Because granite has a lot of naturally occurring silica in its composition, quarry workers whose jobs brought them into regular contact with the dust from the granite-cutting process were at very high risk for silicosis. John Beattie knew the dangers. In his Guilford quarries, he insisted that the stonecutters who finished the stone work in the open air, thus decreasing dust exposure. His only concession to the workers' need for shelter from the elements was to string a sailcloth roof that was open on all sides. It is reported that his quarry had a much lower incidence of silicosis and consumption (tuberculosis) than other quarries, in which stonecutters worked in sheds with an extremely high concentration of silica dust in air. Later a state law misguidedly required the construction of sheds for all workers. Unfortunately, this had the effect of concentrating the silica dust and thereby greatly increasing the danger of silicosis.

Leonard Page, who as a youngster in the late 1920s worked as a tool boy, commented:

I wouldn't be a stone cutter. They died terrible, terrible deaths. . . . [They were] in the cemetery [by the time they] were 50 years old from eating that stone dust. It was bad enough when they were chiseling with just the hammer, but when the air [drills] came out, and the steam [drills] . . . [the dust] would cut the lungs on them. . . . You heard those poor devils coughing and choking until their lungs would bust and out the blood would go, and they would be dead. One Saturday, when I was working up there, somebody said, 'There's somebody dead up the quarry.' I went up, and it was the shed boss. . . . He took a walk up to the office, and . . . he must have started hemorrhaging in the office because there was a puddle of blood all the way until he got in front of the big shed. . . . He fell face first on it, and there was just a burst of blood from his lung. That's the way those poor fellows died, all of them.

Chronic silicosis is seen in workers who have inhaled relatively low concentrations of silica dust for 10 to 20 years. The accumulated dust causes a tissue reaction that results in the formation of small, whorl-shaped nodules that remain in a worker's lungs throughout his or her entire life. These nodules may have no effect, or they may enlarge, increase in number, and join together. Breathlessness results, and there may be cough and sputum production.

Twenty to thirty percent of all chronic silicosis patients progress to complicated illness. At that stage, fibrous tissue replaces soft lung tissue, restricting the lungs' function and leading to breathlessness, weakness, chest pain, a cough, and sputum production. The patient becomes a respiratory cripple, likely to die of heart failure caused by the lung disease (cor pulmonale), or develop tuberculosis as a complication.

John Opie, whose ancestors came to the United States from Cornwall four generations ago, says: "I think the Cornish were typically the stone cutters. The work was tough and most of them died of silicosis or tuberculosis. I never met my grandfather. He died in '44 or '45 [of lung disease] as I expect his father did before him."

Sometimes workers exposed to considerable silica dust over a short period of time—such as drillers, polishers, and sandblasters—develop acute silicosis. *Acute silicosis* is rapidly progressive, as unremediable as lung cancer, disabling, and often fatal within five years. The disease is characterized by difficulty in breathing, loss of weight, fever, and coughing. The alveoli (breathing spaces in the lungs) become inflamed, and fibrosis (scar tissue) rapidly develops in the lungs. Many sufferers of acute silicosis were young, active people. When tuberculosis was more common, it often occurred as a complication of silicosis. The Government's Ninth Report on Carcinogens, released in 2000, also cites silica as a known carcinogen. People with silicosis have two to four times the incidence of lung cancer of those without.

To prevent silicosis, dust control must be implemented. This may mean wetting down worksites and improving ventilation, or providing special suits and breathing apparatus to workers exposed to silica. It was many years before these preventive measures were instituted in the quarries of the United States.

Accident, injury, or quarry worker's disease—such was the lot of many a quarry worker in the industry's glory days. Tragically, the magnificent output of the quarries was tarnished by the cost in human suffering.

—MZ

STEAM AND RAIL

When steam power changed the world, it altered the business of quarrying forever. Steam power made it possible to build machinery of immense potential, which in turn moved people with greater speed and in greater numbers. And it made it possible— even necessary—for people to migrate to where the machines operated in swelling cities full of growing businesses.

In the 1780s, James Watt patented developments for the steam engine that greatly expanded its usefulness. By 1807, Robert Fulton was powering a steamship on the Hudson, and by 1829, George Stevenson had developed a powerful version of a steam locomotive. In 1800, just 65,000 people lived in New York City. By 1850, that number had swelled to 500,000, and by 1880, to 1.1 million. In 1900, the population of New York City reached three million souls.

With burgeoning city populations all across the United States came the urgent need for fireproof construction material. Quarrying stone became big business, and Stony Creek's proximity to railroad, tidal water, and New York City made it an ideal quarry site for the era.

Steam power arrived in the quarries during their heyday of the 1880s and 1890s. Workers were now assisted, defined, and imperiled by pneumatic tools, spinning crankshafts, powerful cranes, and pressured steam boilers. In their own

way, quarry companies became industrial organizations with well-defined jobs, a social hierarchy, long hours, company-based housing, and labor unions. But electricity and the telephone were still decades away. Quarry workers depended on the light of day filtering into stonecutting sheds from windows that ran the length of the buildings.

Between 1870 and 1890, six new major quarries opened in the Stony Creek area, along with a host of small pits that stonecutters hewed for themselves in their own back yards. The Pine Orchard Quarry and Beattie's Quarries on Leete's Island both opened in 1870. Beattie's Quarries grew to be one of the two largest operations in the area—rivaled in size only by the Norcross Brothers Quarry, which opened in 1882. At their peaks, Beattie and Norcross each employed nearly 700 workers.

The next largest quarry, Brooklyn Quarry, east of Prospect Hill, opened in the 1880s and

105

Norcross Brothers
Quarry

closed in the 1890s, employing more than 150 workers at its height of operation. The quarry got its name from the fact that most of its stone was sold to Brooklyn, New York, for use in paving and breakwaters. Other quarries of that period bore the names Red Hill, Hanna, Opie, Keats-Barber, Murphy's, and Tom Dyer's.

Beattie and Norcross stand out as prototypical. Beattie's was the largest of the early tidewater quarry operations, but Norcross and its contemporaries managed to operate successfully farther inland by employing rail spurs that connected them with the coast. Both quarries ultimately relied on schooners and the railroad for transporting their stone, and both used similar extraction and cutting processes. Local historian Liza Carroll writes:

A list of equipment at the [Norcross Brothers] quarry is as descriptive as anything can be of the enormous enterprise it was at its height in the late nineteenth century. There were nine cranes, each one capable of lifting 45 tons [40.5 t] of stone, a main shed and side sheds for dynamite, carpentry, lathes, stone saws, tools, and polishing. There [were] an office . . . boiler room, generators, a drafting building, a livery stable, two boardinghouses, an engine house for locomotives, a freight station, a dock, two locomotives, and five miles [8 km] of track.

TWO DERRICKS
The spidery apparatus is called a *guy-wire derrick.* The central pole, made of wood, was held in place by wires that were anchored to the ground up on the hill. The metal derrick, also called the *stiff-leg derrick,* was the newer of the two. It was self-supporting and could rotate from about 180 to 270 degrees.

WORK METHODS

Harnessing the power of the steam engine to lift and move newly freed blocks of stone required a vantage point well above the stone to be quarried. So the quarries erected towering wooden masts called *derricks*—poles that stood over 100 feet (30.5 m) tall—and guyed them into place at the top of the face to be excavated. Once a block had been cut, workers belted a chain around the block, then lowered a cable from a boom on the derrick and attached it to the chain. They hoisted the block, swung the boom, and either relayed the block to the next derrick or lowered it directly onto a railcar.

This means of moving the extracted stone meant that it was easier to excavate vertically— going ever deeper down the rock face—so that the derrick would not have to be moved. For this reason, beginning in the late nineteenth century, quarries became deep pits in the ground.

The extraction process itself was still a matter of drilling a line of holes and applying a wedging force. But now, hand drills had given way to steam drills and wedges had given way to "slow" explosives like black powder—at least for the excavation process. Quarrymen continued to use plugs and feathers for the sizing-down splits.

Finding the grain along which to blast and hew the stone was not easy. Granite does not show a grain as readily as sandstone and other sedimentary stone. Experienced quarrymen actually developed the ability to feel the grain. As Anthony "Unk" DaRos relates:

After a while, if you have been working with a stone long enough, you could tell the grain. The average person couldn't tell the grain. But I can tell the grain by feeling it. I learned that trick from the old-timers. They were so tough, those old-timers. They could do it, and I always thought they were showing off. You would wonder how they could feel anything because their hands were like rawhide, they were so tough. I learned

that by feeling you could actually tell the grain of it. In fact, you can't tell by looking at it. You would have to actually feel it.

Once the grain was discerned, black powder was inserted into a line of holes and set off. A series of powder blasts could free a block 70 feet (21.3 m) long, 60 feet (18.3 m) wide, and 35 feet (10.7 m) deep. Quarrymen preferred black powder over dynamite because it could open a seam with relatively little damage, whereas dynamite shattered the stone.

After freeing and sizing the blocks, quarrymen moved the stone by a series of wooden derricks—the engineer's mythical

"sky hooks"—either to railroad tracks built into
the quarries, or onto a big "sled" pulled by a team
of oxen. Given the tremendous weight of the
stone being moved, one might wonder why the
quarries used derricks of wood rather than of
steel. Folklore has it that the wooden masts were
preferred because the wood gave forewarning of
its imminent failure with a whip-snapping
crackle, whereas a steel derrick might bend
suddenly without a sound.

The blocks were brought to stonecutters for
finishing. The cutting shed at the Norcross

Quarry was about 100 feet (30.5 m) long, with a
spinning shaft running overhead down its center.
Stonecutters were the most highly skilled—and
highest paid—of the quarry workers. To be able
to work on a piece of stone, they would fix it in a
plaster base so it could not move. In the early
years, they worked with hand points and chisels,
and later with pneumatic tools to smooth and
shape each piece of granite.

Steel tools were used for cutting and shaping
the stone, and these tools required frequent
sharpening. With scores of stonecutters working

in a quarry, several blacksmiths could be busy full time, sharpening tools and forging new ones as tools wore down beyond honing. At its peak, Norcross had 28 blacksmiths on its payroll. Each blacksmith had his own tool boy who would shuttle the tools in a wire basket between cutter and blacksmith. Many sons of quarrymen began their own careers in the quarry as tool boys.

Once the stone was cut to its prescribed dimensions, it might require polishing. The polishing process involved using perforated discs that were 2 to 3 feet (0.6 to 0.9 m) in diameter. The discs were turned by means of belts that connected the discs to the cutting shed's central spinning shaft. Steam power kept the shaft turning, and cutters would engage and disengage the polishing discs by engaging and disengaging the belt. The discs were perforated with tiny grooves into which a cutter poured progressively smaller steel shot that ground the stone's surface. After the smallest shot had done its work, the cutter would apply garnet dust, which formed a sort of putty. The finishing step was to apply a very fine grit called "putty powder" to put a fine polish on the surface. Most of the finished products needed to be protected, so carpenters built individual wooden crates for shipping each piece.

The process of extracting, splitting, and cutting produced a great deal of stone that could not be used as dimension stone. This waste—estimated by some to be as much as 80 percent of what was extracted—was thrown into high piles of what was called *riprap* or *grout*. Alternatively, it could be used in breakwaters or seawalls.

—RD

THE BLACKSMITH SHOP
The blacksmith kept a constant supply of tools ready for the quarrymen. The steel tools then in use needed to be tempered with heat to make them hard but not brittle. Modern tools have carbide tips, which do not need to be tempered. Young boys worked as runners, delivering the tools to workers all over the quarry.

AN INDUSTRY IN CONTINUAL CRISIS

Even in the age that coined the term *cutthroat competition,* the granite industry stood out as unstable and chancy. Unlike some minerals, such as coal and iron, which could only be found in select locations, granite was extraordinarily common. Furthermore, because quarrying did not require expensive machinery or sophisticated engineering, costs of entering the industry were relatively low. By the 1880s, hundreds of quarries, large and small, were operating throughout New England, from the islands of Maine's Penobscot Bay to southern Connecticut to Vermont and New Hampshire (long nicknamed "the Granite State").

Some industries, because of the nature of the technologies they employ or the character of their markets, lend themselves to consolidation. Entrepreneurs such as John D. Rockefeller and his associates—who had access to significant capital—might consolidate petroleum commerce, for example, by controlling the refining, transportation, and marketing of the product. They would then integrate backward to control the sources of supply, as well. The consolidation of other industries—food and tobacco, rubber, primary metals, lumber, chemicals, paper, glass, and machinery—followed a similar pattern, taking advantage both of national demands for standardized products and of economies of scale. The granite industry was not amenable to consolidation.

Consumers of granite (government agencies, architects, construction firms) did not generally demand uniform products like "pavers" or "curbstones," but customized ones—elements crafted for particular buildings or structures. Thus the industry could not use mass production techniques that created economies of scale and lowered production costs. Even had the industry adopted mass production technologies, its unpredictable and contract-dependent market would not have produced significant economies. The instability of the market also precluded the industry's benefiting from rebates and volume discounts that mass producers of other products could extract from railroads and steamship companies.

Ultimately, the granite industry was able to consolidate in only a few areas. In certain regions, groups of quarry owners who controlled the sources of certain kinds of stone managed to fix prices and squeeze out competitors. (For example, Maine had a notorious and politically powerful "Granite Ring" in the 1880s and 1890s.) But even these arrangements seldom lasted long because the financial incentives for cheating one's co-conspirators were too great.

The most successful consolidations occurred in marketing. Demands by contractors and architects for wide varieties of stone encouraged the growth of dealerships like the New York- and Chicago-based John Pierce Company. In the 1906 edition of *Sweet's Indexed Catalogue of Building Construction,* John Pierce offered granite from such well-known quarries as:

Hallowell Granite Works. Hallowell, Maine.
   White, fine grained.
Bodwell Granite Company. (Fox Island). Vinal
   Haven, Maine. Warm gray, close grained.
Mount Waldo Granite Works. Frankfort, Maine.
   Light gray, fine and coarse grained.
Spruce Head Quarry. Spruce Head, Maine. Gray,
   close grained.

Jonesboro Quarry. Jonesboro, Maine. Brown-
   red, close grained.
Stony Creek Red Granite Co. Stony Creek,
   Conn. Red-mottled, coarse grained.

The advertisement went on to list impressive public and private buildings in New York, Chicago, Washington, Ohio, and Wisconsin in which stone from these quarries had been used and concluded by inviting correspondence from architects and builders "to whom estimates and prices will be furnished upon request." While far from regularizing this tumultuous industry, such arrangements unquestionably introduced important elements of order to the marketing process.

As the industry evolved, markets for certain kinds of granite products did eventually lend themselves to mass production. After granite began to be replaced by reinforced concrete as a structural stone, it found its eventual niche as a decorative material. By the turn of the century, monument makers, working through their national trade association, were promoting standardized designs and materials that could be produced using mass production techniques. This led to the concentration of monument manufacturing by firms such as Vermont's Rock of Ages consortium.

Stony Creek granite

From *Modern Memorial Art,* a promotional booklet of The Dodds Granite Company

On the bleak shore of Long Island Sound, near the village of Stony Creek, in New Haven County, Connecticut, there jut forth massive and rugged outcroppings of an unusual and distinctive granite.

Untiring Time has registered the tides of countless centuries upon these granite giants without obliterating or in any wise impairing the beauty and glory of variegated yet harmonious coloring which adorns their naked heads. In vain have the blinding storms and biting cold of numberless New England winters assailed these ridges of adamantine rock. They have remained materially unaltered from age to age.

Today, in city parks, on public squares and in places of the greatest prominence, the products of these quarries, fashioned into fitting forms of classic beauty and elegance, keep endless vigil at the shrine of the Nation's Immortals; while in our cemeteries, everywhere, appear examples of the individual charm that may invest a private memorial, whose delicate warmth of coloring so beautifully betokens the depth and sincerity of the tenderness that prompts each silent tribute to the dead.

"Stony Creek" commends itself as a granite quite impervious to climatic influences, and of surpassing beauty. Its soft shades of pink and green, of brown and gray, so perfectly blended or so strikingly contrasted, patterned in most superb mottling and veining by the mystic hand of Nature, are the wonder and delight of America's greatest artists, whose masterpieces are in this wonderful material.

Our quarries and plants at Stony Creek are developed and adequately equipped to meet promptly and efficiently any requirement in this granite.

The inability of granite producers to reduce competition through consolidation gave the industry a uniquely unstable character that affected not only its workforce, but also the communities in which it operated. Despite technological developments that mechanized important parts of the task of producing finished granite, the industry remained unusually labor-intensive—dependent both on highly skilled cadres of carvers, powdermen, blacksmiths, and mechanics and on gangs of unskilled laborers. Because work was seasonal and contract-driven, these workers tended to move from quarry to quarry up and down the coast, wherever contracts had been awarded. Inevitably, competition between workers for jobs was as intense as competition between companies for contracts. Labor unions tried as early as the 1870s to introduce some order into this process by requiring "traveling cards" of all members who wished to move on. The cards would give them *entree* to jobs once they had reached their destinations. The card system was nearly impossible to enforce, however, because of the constant influx of new non-union workers into the labor pool. Needless to say, the surplus of migrant, non-union labor delighted the quarry owners, who had been driven to lowering costs of production by lowering wages. The owners

eventually sought to foment tensions between various ethnic groups, union and non-union workers, and skilled and unskilled workers, in order to discourage labor organization.

Broad economic forces further aggravated relations between employers and employees. Between 1873 and 1896, America's economy was in the grips of a long-term deflationary spiral. This squeezed businessmen who had borrowed money in inflated dollars, since their loans had to be repaid out of diminishing incomes. This, plus unrestrained competition, forced employers to constantly seek to lower costs, and—whether for a railroad company, a steel manufacturer, or a granite quarry—labor costs proved to be the most flexible. Wages could be lowered, hours of work lengthened, and production schedules sped up. And there was very little that workers could do about it, since they could so easily be replaced.

Quarry workers' union meeting

Unions and strikes

The quarry workers were one of the earliest groups to organize and unionize. The Granite Cutters International Association was formed in 1877 in Maine for better wages and working conditions. In 1886, the Barre, Vermont, workers, with Scots taking the lead, formed what was to become the largest and most influential branch of them all. They wanted to shorten the 10-hour workday on Saturdays. Stony Creek workers at Norcross Brothers Quarry affiliated with this national union in 1890 "for a thorough organization of the trade." Workers in other area quarries probably did so at the same time, or shortly thereafter. Handbooks appeared in both English and Italian. And in 1897, workers at Beattie's Quarries went on strike.

Anarchists and socialists brought critical mass and energy to the early union movement. Anarchists opposed all forms of established government. Individuals should have the freedom to express themselves, they believed, unhindered by any repression or control by government, business, church, or authority. In theory, they justified political assassination and terrorism under the conviction that political leaders were "enemies of the people."

Socialists called for public or state ownership and control of the production and distribution of wealth. At the turn of the century in the United States, socialists sought to reconstruct the capitalist system through strong trade unions and new laws. They contended that oppression of workers could be corrected peacefully if workers would unite, organize, and demand changes in work laws, pay, and factory conditions.

Mistreated, poorly paid workers were understandably attracted to socialism, and some to anarchism. Because both systems were in essence anti-capitalist—and viewed by many as anti-religious, anti-American imports from Europe—they terrified both the Protestant tycoons and the general public. People justifiably came to fear the violence that the strikes too often engendered.

In the coal-mining areas of Pennsylvania, terrorist groups sprang up among Irish-born miners, the poorest and most exploited of American workers. In the Railroad Strike of 1877, more than 1,000 miners went on strike, leading to the violent burning of some 2,000 railroad cars, yards, warehouses, and factories, and nine deaths. When state militias could not contain the violence, Federal troops were ordered into Pennsylvania, West Virginia, Maryland, and Illinois by President Rutherford B. Hayes. Meanwhile, in the West, hostility broke out against Chinese immigrants in an anti-immigrant frenzy of retaliation.

A decade later, in 1886, violence erupted in Chicago's Haymarket Square Riot. It began when between 40,000 and 60,000 trade unionists laid down their tools in support of an eight-hour workday. Violence broke out at the McCormick Harvesting Machine Company. Two men were killed, and half a dozen injured. The following day, labor leaders convened what was intended as a peaceful protest meeting. When police ordered them to disperse, someone threw a bomb (no one ever discovered who), instantly killing a police officer and fatally wounding six demonstrators. Police fired into the crowd, and another four people died. Circulars later called for "Revenge! Workingmen! To Arms!" citing Haymarket Square as "the latest atrocious acts of the police." Later seven policemen and 10 workmen were killed and 50 injured.

The Pullman Strike made national headlines in 1894. George Pullman had amassed a fortune in manufacturing sleeper, dining, and chair cars for the railroads. In 1880, he built the town of Pullman, Illinois, as a model industrial community on the shore of Lake Michigan, away from the grime and degradation of Chicago. He required his workers to live in his model town and pay rent to the company. One embittered employee colorfully described life there: "We are born in a Pullman house, fed from the Pullman shop, taught in the Pullman school, catechized in the Pullman church, and when we die we shall be buried in the Pullman cemetery and go to the Pullman hell."

Eugene Debs, the hated union organizer and socialist, successfully unionized Pullman workers and organized a strike in 1894 that spread to 27 states, paralyzing freight in and out of Chicago. Mob activity and riots ensued, causing President Grover Cleveland to send in Federal troops: infantry, artillery, cavalry, and 3,600 Federal marshals.

The assassination of President William McKinley in 1901 in Buffalo, New York, once again sent the nation into a crisis. He was ➤

Unions and strikes *(continued)*

shot and killed by an anarchist, Leon Czolgosz, son of Polish immigrants and a wire mill worker. To the average citizen, anarchism came to mean real, violent, lawless disorder, not just polemical theory. The cornerstone of the Stony Creek Congregational Church, laid two weeks after the assassination, contains much memorabilia pertaining to "our martyred President."

Most workers were not wild-eyed, bomb-throwing anarchists trying to overthrow the government. They did not have much time for economic theory. They were average people seeking bread and butter, better pay, decent homes, and education for their children. They saw unions as roads to a better life.

No violence of this magnitude occurred in the Stony Creek area in either of the quarry strikes of 1892 or 1900. However, local quarry workers maintained close ties to the national quarry workers' union out of Barre, Vermont, and they were certainly exposed to national publications, traveling speakers, and union dogma. Barre itself became a hotbed of union and socialist agitation. The Socialist Labor Party there, formed largely by Italian workers, built a socialist hall, complete with the arm and hammer medallion on its portal. The region's quarry workers traveled regularly among centers of work, and local union leaders made sure their members remained well informed on what needed to be done.

In the Great Lockout Strike of 1892, which began in May and continued for five months, the union demanded piecework rate changes and a nine-hour workday. Most of the quarry workers in New England (numbering more than 10,000) went out on strike. Local records refer to the strike, but give few details of its effect. Gertrude McKenzie, who noted that the "strike so crippled business that it never resumed its former proportions," may have been referring to a particular quarry or to another strike in 1900.

The Norcross workers reluctantly supported the Strike of 1900, a general strike in New England. According to newspaper reports, cutters were asking for 35 cents an hour and an eight-hour workday. Several manufacturers had compromised with workers against the dictates of the national union. Norcross and Beattie agreed to 33 and 34 cents an hour respectively and the eight-hour workday. The strike began on March 1. By March 29, some were working again.

By mid-April, 80 workmen, including 52 cutters, had returned to work.

The national union of stonecutters notified the local union that they did not approve of a five-year contract and the wage agreement. The men were ordered to quit work. But the workers bucked the union and kept working. The national union demanded the local union's charter. In response, the locals notified the secretary of the union that "if he wanted the charter, to come up and get it. Up to date he has not put in an appearance." They criticized the union official with being "very officious" regarding the settlement between Norcross and the union. A union official from New Haven came out to demand the surrender of the charter if they refused to stop working. Finally, and with a great deal of reluctance, they stopped work, not wanting to be banned by the national union and lose other important benefits. Although workers were not willing to surrender the charter, and therefore resumed striking, they needed to work.

The second and final settlement took place in May between Norcross and the union for 33 and 35 cents an hour for an eight-hour day, with an increase of 14 percent for piecework, to run for three years, not five.

In the final analysis, declines in the demand for granite because of newer building methods and materials had a far greater impact on the decline of quarrying after the turn of the century than did the strikes. In 1904, only Norcross is listed in the Branford Business Directory. Directories for 1909, 1915, 1917, and 1920 list the Norcross and Stony Creek Red Granite Companies. In 1925, Dodds, formerly Norcross, is the only one listed. Beattie's Quarries in Guilford ceased operations in 1918. Sachem's Head Quarry struggled on with several owners, closing for good in 1911. Some quarry workers looked elsewhere for work. Some moved away. Several men went to work at the Malleable Iron Fittings Company, the local wire mill, and Yale & Towne Manufacturing Company in Branford.

—WJ

TROUBLED TIMES:

THE NOT-SO-GAY NINETIES

The early 1890s proved to be particularly troubled years for American labor in general and for the granite industry in particular. The climax of this troubled era was the Great Lockout (or Strike, depending on the side one chose) of 1892. The dispute centered on disagreement over the expiration dates of the "bills of prices," by which quarrymen annually agreed on rates for their work. Quarrymen were not paid wages but piecework rates based on the costs of completing certain jobs. Traditionally, these rates had been set in May, after most sales contracts—which were usually signed early in the year—had been made. The May date gave workers the advantage in the bargaining process, since they could figure prices on the basis of a known volume of work and the cash value of the contracts. In 1892, the quarry owners decided to shift the expiration date to the end of the calendar year. This would enable them to figure bids with labor costs already fixed, and so offset the possibility of strikes in their busiest season.

In May of 1892, when the National Granite Cutters Union and the Granite Manufacturers Association of New England failed to reach agreement on bills of prices, most of the quarry workers in the region set down their tools. In some places, workers and their families were evicted from company-owned housing. In places like the Maine islands, where all purchases were made at company-owned stores, storekeepers shut off lines of credit and closed their doors to strikers. Some employers brought in strikebreakers—who were sometimes, but not always, "dissuaded" from getting the quarries running again. Though the strikers could live off garden plots and hunt and fish through the summer, by fall, the union's will began to weaken. In September, a conference between the union and the employers' association produced a compromise on the date for setting bills of prices (March) and established arbitration mechanisms for the settlement of other disputes.

Labor troubles in the industry did not end. The national financial panic in 1893, which helped to spark a national railroad strike and a deep business depression, curtailed major building projects and led to thousands of layoffs in every industry. The granite labor agreement ran through 1895. As soon as it terminated, labor and capital were again locked in battle, with periodic work stoppages in quarries up and down the East Coast. Unrest in the granite industry joined a much larger mobilization of urban and agrarian radicals. These activists took control of the Democratic Party in 1896, demanding government control of banks and railroads and an income tax, as well as urging capitalists, in the words of William Jennings Bryan, not to "crucify mankind upon a cross of gold nor press down upon the brow of labor a crown of thorns."

Wealth won the electoral struggle against commonwealth in 1896, thanks to the first modern national political campaign, organized by Cleveland industrialist and U.S. senator Marcus Alonzo Hanna. Yet steps would have to be taken to put an end to the labor strife that had plagued the nation since the 1870s. The industrial interests devised a carrot and stick strategy. On the carrot side, capital adopted a more conciliatory rhetoric, advocated arbitration of disputes, and in many places, initiated corporate-sponsored welfare and education programs (later termed "welfare capitalism"). On the stick side, they notched up the search for production and management techniques that would simplify manufacturing processes in order to disempower the skilled workers who were the backbone of organized labor. Since no technology existed to automate the skilled work of the granite industry, employers sought alternative building methods. It is no coincidence that Frederick Winslow Taylor—the "father" of scientific management techniques that effectively deskilled the metals-

fabricating industries—was also one of the leading promoters of the reinforced-concrete construction methods that eventually eliminated many skilled workers in the building trades.

Ultimately, continuing competition in the granite industry succeeded in squeezing out many smaller firms, primarily because efficient operations required increasingly expensive machinery. The extent of basic equipment needed for even a small quarrying operation is suggested by the inventory if items seized by authorities when the Breakwater Construction Company of Cleveland, Ohio, defaulted on its mortgage in 1911. The equipment listed included:

steel railways, 1.9 miles
1 Baldwin class 22 a-1 locomotive
20 flat and dump cars
1 250 horsepower type aa-1 Ingersoll-Rand two stage
    air compressor, complete on foundations
1 200 horsepower type a-1 Ingersoll-Rand single stage
    air compressor
60 sets of wheels
9 double cylinder double drum hoisting machines
1 rotary swinging engine and gear
9 derricks, 15 to 25 ton capacity with 50–80 foot masts,
    45 to 95 foot booms
8 boilers
2 vertical tubular boilers

121

1 complete blacksmith shop equipment, with forges, air
     blasts, and power hammers, anvils, cutters, etc.
5 Ingersoll-Rand air drills
3 Ingersoll-Rand baby air drills
2 pneumatic hammer drills
about 5.25 miles of air and water pipes
4 steam pumps
2 water tanks
2 steel tank air receivers
2 heaters
2 hydraulic lifting jacks
1 Fairbanks standard track and car scale
2 hydraulic giant nozzles
1 stone crusher
2 coal hoisting tubs
3 horsepower hoists
18 sets of stone chains & hooks (with capacity for
     lifting up to 25 tons)
10 wheelbarrows
3 heavy draught horses
2 wagons
2 sets of harness
2 carriages

All picks, shovels, crowbars, car-replacers, tongs,
small tools in quarry, blacksmith shop, machine shop,
carpenter shop, spikes, ties, steel rail, wire rod, dynamite,
powder, coal hardware, iron and steel rods, castings, etc.,
journal boxes, car brasses, lanterns, manila rope, pipe

fittings, valves, drill parts and repair parts for other
machinery, bolts, washers, nuts, packing, etc., covering
the tools and supplies on hand, in store room and in use
in and about the Company's quarry at Sachem's Head.

Extensive as the inventory sounds, this was a
very simple quarry operation that sold rough
stone for jetties. It couldn't compare to far more
elaborate plants such as that maintained by Stony
Creek's Norcross Brothers Quarry. To produce
finished architectural elements, the Norcross
operation required power-driven polishing
machines, a stone lathe for turning columns,
stone saws, and other specialized devices.

By the turn of the century, only big
operations with the most sophisticated
equipment, control of the best stone, access to
inexpensive transportation, and contacts with the
most aggressive dealers, could hope to survive.
By 1920, only one of the nine quarries that had
operated in and around Stony Creek was still in
operation—and that on a scale very much
reduced from its glory days, when it had
employed between 600 and 700 men.

—PDH

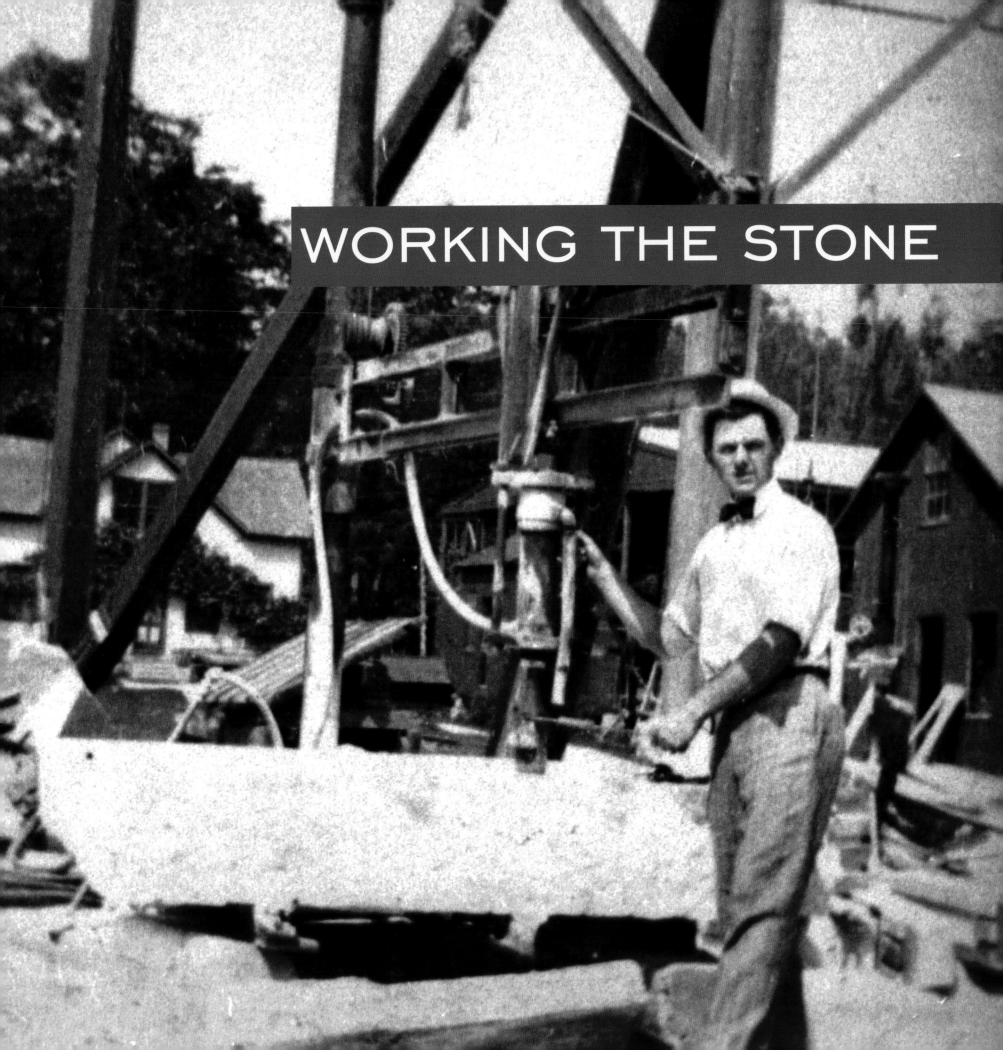

WORKING THE STONE

Life was harsh. Stony Creek pink granite

offered no romance and scant beauty for those who worked stone

weighing in at about 165 pounds per cubic foot (2,493 kg/m^3).

Climbing a 135-foot (41.1-meter) derrick to grease gears could be

frightening and dangerous. And setting a charge to blast stone from

the earth required a peculiar sort of courage. Skilled or not, quarry

workers daily faced a punishing routine that sent them home

exhausted at best. In the worst case, Doc Townsend came running

to treat the mangled fingers and crushed toes—or to pronounce

someone beyond help. One and all knew the symptoms of silicosis,

the quarryman's lung disease, because they daily saw it in action

all around them.

The men stayed in heatless boardinghouses. In addition, in the

quarries' heyday, many people in town rented rooms to the

workers. When the workers migrated to other regions in search of steady work, they left struggling families behind and sent paltry paychecks home. Eventually, most of the workers moved on, but there were some who settled in Stony Creek. Mostly immigrants—Scots, Irish, Cornish, Italians, Finns, and Swedes—they changed the face of the village. Many liked to drink and kept Stony Creek's saloons thriving. They also held on to lifestyles and religions from the Old Country that scandalized their Yankee hosts.

Despite all, the quarry workers found a certain dignity in what they did. They posed proudly on quarry cliffs for photographs, although few smiled. They stood a little taller when work was sent off to New York, Boston, Washington, Caracas, Paris, London, or Havana. And when the 41-foot (12.5-meter) monolith was shipped by train to West Point for the future Battle Monument, they watched it depart with great fanfare.

The workers wanted 33 cents an hour for their 10-hour, six-day work week. While the quarry unions helped, they and other unions were as controversial then as issues of race, homosexuality, and abortion are today. Fair business practice and the rights of workers became entangled with religion, ethnicity, lifestyle, and economics. Strikes flared up and sometimes turned nasty.

Even so, the quarrymen made the best of it. And they made music. Some families organized gatherings around pianos to sing. Accordions were commonplace in the village. The Stony Creek Band, organized by quarry workers, had over 20 members. Band members stood with their heads held high in their braided uniforms and flat-topped hats, displaying their drums and brass pieces.

Some of the quarrymen cut, crafted, and polished granite in their spare time. Sometimes they sold polished granite balls or gave them as gifts. And they left a legacy of their doodles on rock faces that later showed up as foundation stones and front stoops or simply remained where they had been worked: in the woods, in a quarry waste pile, or in someone's yard. The work of the quarry was hard, but stone was the quarry workers' life.

—WJ

"OLD HOLE" IN THE SOUTHERN SECTION OF THE DODDS GRANITE COMPANY QUARRY (NOVEMBER 6, 1925)
The Old Hole remained active until 1987. After that, Castellucci (owners as of the mid-1950s) moved operations to a new section in the quarry's northern portion. The large block of granite that appears in the foreground of both photographs has just been blasted out of the ledge. The workmen may have miscalculated and used too much black powder; it appears that the stone nearly hit the derrick.

QUARRY WORKERS

Seated, from left, top row: Charles Nichols, Ed Whalen, Nick Mullen, Weymouth Davy; middle row: Ed Fay, Donald McMullen, Frank Hair, George Walker; bottom row: ? Smith. Standing around tree, from left: James Roach, Chris Beebe, W. Casey, Terry Divine, Sam Barnes

Quarry workers in front of quarry office

QUARRY LEDGE (1981)
Modern machinery
replaced the old derricks.

ENGINE ROOM
Jack Barnes ran the derrick
from the engine room.
This building still stands at
the quarry today, one of
the few survivors from the
quarry's earlier days.

DERRICKS
Both the guy-wire and the stiff-leg derrick are visible in this photograph.

SETTING THE
"DOGS" AND
LOADING THE STONE
The tools seen
gripping the stone
in these pictures
are called *dogs*.
Each stone was
numbered (above).
The "R" indicates
the direction of
the rift. The "H"
indicates that the
block came from
the head grain.

134

Stony Creek granite was used to build abutments for the piers that support the George Washington Bridge. *Above:* The barge *Molly Dodds* unloading granite blocks on the shore of the Hudson River in 1927. The granite came out of Dodds Quarry in Stony Creek and was loaded onto barges at the oyster dock on Flying Point.

Granite blocks unloaded on shore

One pier is now nearly complete and awaiting construction of the bridge tower atop it.

A friendly visit to the
quarry's engine

THE MAIN OFFICE AT THE QUARRY
Visiting dignitaries often slept on the second floor, above the quarry offices.

MEN ON THE LEDGE
The triple drill holes visible in the wall behind the men resulted from an old drilling technique.

The Dodds Granite Co.
quarry in Stony Creek,
circa 1920s

AN EXPLOSION
Until the 1950s, quarry workers used black powder to blow huge blocks of granite out of the ledge.
This dangerous technique, which was hard to calculate accurately, caused many accidents and wasted a lot of stone.
Today workers use hydraulic and pneumatic drills instead.

BUILT TO LAST

BUILDINGS, MONUMENTS, AND STRUCTURES

The story of Stony Creek granite is in part the story of dreamers and creators. Although Connecticut has never been a leader in mineral production, some of the best-known structures to be built over the last 150 years utilize the state's pink granite. As engineers, architects, and memorial builders conceived of architecture that would both endure and meet the changing needs of a nation, Stony Creek granite became a building block intrinsic to their visions.

Osborn Hall, built on Yale University's Old Campus in 1888, was one of the first to use Stony Creek pink granite from the Norcross Brothers Quarry. The building was razed in 1926.

The igneous rock that has come to be known as *Stony Creek granite* ranges from Long Island Sound inland about 3.5 miles (5.6 km) along the coast of Connecticut, from Haycock Point in Branford to the West River in Guilford. Approximately 6 miles (9.7 km) in length, the irregular semicircular granite formation has a geologic history hundreds of millions of years old. Yet Stony Creek granite has been successfully quarried in Branford and Guilford only since the late 1850s, particularly in the Branford village of Stony Creek. The stone's durability and beauty have brought it great popularity as an architectural material—it appears in prominent buildings in cities as far from home as Montreal, Canada; New Orleans, Louisiana; Cumberland, Maryland; and Cincinnati, Ohio. It features in major monuments found in such diverse places as

Exeter, New Hampshire; Hattiesburg, Mississippi; Wichita, Kansas; and Los Angeles, California; and internationally in Santiago, Cuba; London, England; and Caracas, Venezuela. In addition, it has been used in abundance in bridges, breakwaters, and other utilitarian structures concentrated in southern New England and New York State.

Stony Creek granite owes its market success to more than beauty and versatility. Building trends, changing styles, economic considerations, and immigration patterns have all played their part. Yet it is the stone's unique aesthetic qualities and its ability to inspire that have brought it international acclaim.

THE QUARRIES AT THEIR HEIGHT

The heyday of Stony Creek quarrying (1870 to 1900) coincided with the rise of the architectural

143

profession in the United States. Young practitioners received instruction as early as 1865 at the Massachusetts Institute of Technology in Cambridge; others attended Columbia University in New York City, or studied at the era's premier school of architecture: the École des Beaux Arts in Paris, France. At the École, students absorbed a strong stylistic emphasis on classical precedents embellished with decorative detailing. They also learned the tenets of effective city planning, including spatial relationships between buildings. These principles were embodied in the monumental City Beautiful plan and Beaux Arts building styles chosen for the 1893 World's Columbian Exposition in Chicago, Illinois. Although it was the nature of the event to be temporary, the principles applied there went on to influence the design of North America's finest late nineteenth- and early twentieth-century public buildings and their settings.

In that same period, prominent American architects often chose to use Stony Creek granite, a material well-suited to the neoclassicism of the era. Sparkling with feldspar, the stone's attractive pink color humanized the stately architectural styles in vogue for churches, fraternal organizations, hospitals, museums, libraries, government offices, and educational institutions,

as well as for banks, hotels, railroad terminals, and office and loft buildings.

Stony Creek granite quarries also provided stonework for hundreds of memorial structures erected throughout the United States and abroad. Many well-known, late nineteenth- and early twentieth-century sculptors and architectural firms collaborated in creating a corpus of lasting monuments to prominent individuals, military heroes, and significant historical events. Partially or wholly built of granite, these structures took various forms, including but not limited to statues on pedestals, memorial tablets, tombs, cemetery gateways, fountains, and flagpoles.

Branford and Guilford quarries also provided stone for numerous engineering landmarks built in southern New England and New York State, as well as other locales along the Atlantic seaboard. Stony Creek granite's strength, durability, and convenient availability made it especially appealing for the construction of various types of bridges, breakwaters, walls, and wharves in the Northeast.

Guilford's Beattie's Quarries alone supplied tons of granite for many structures built between 1870 and 1915. Early projects in New York included the city's first street curbing, the northern half of Battery Wharf, the granite foundations and abutments for the Brooklyn

Bridge, and the Harlem River Tunnel. In Connecticut, Beattie stonework went into bridges over the Connecticut, Housatonic, and Thames Rivers, and breakwaters in Greenwich (Cos Cob), Bridgeport, New Haven, Old Saybrook, and Clinton. Beattie supplied stone to Massachusetts for two bridges crossing the Connecticut River in Springfield and for a breakwater in Westport, and in the same period supplied Rhode Island projects, that included granite foundations for a beacon at Wickford Harbor in North Kingston and the Old Harbor Breakwater on Block Island. Beattie's Quarries also provided granite state boundary markers for Massachusetts, New Jersey, New York, Pennsylvania, and Vermont, and stonework for a grain elevator in Newport News, Virginia— believed to be the largest on the East Coast when completed in 1876.

A CENTURY LATER

In 1976, as the demand for granite decreased, the Castellucci & Sons, Inc. firm of Providence, Rhode Island, sold its 450-acre (180-hectare) holding in Stony Creek to the Town of Branford, although a long-term lease enabled the small, family-owned company to continue operating this last surviving quarry for commercial purposes. While business was slow during

The extent of Stony Creek granite

March 31, 1983

Dear Mr. Castellucci:

At your request I was asked to determine the extent of Stony Creek granite within the confines of your property. . . .

The amount of stone that can be quarried within the property boundaries is considerable. A stone block (representing only a portion of the property) 1,000 feet long, 100 feet wide, and 80 feet deep would yield 6,800,000 cubic feet of stone after 15% has been subtracted for not meeting standards. At the present rate of production of about 100,000 cubic feet of stone a year the block above would yield more granite than can be quarried in the next 50 years.

August 29, 1989

. . . The 7.5 acre present working area is entirely underlain by Stony Creek granite and represents 326,700 square feet (1 acre = 43,560 square). The working face is 120 feet high which gives the stone mass a volume of 39,204,000 cubic feet. At the present extraction rate of 15,000 cubic feet a month, quarrying at the 7.5 acre site can proceed for 2,613 months.

Yours truly,
Sidney Horenstein
Geologist

the late 1970s, granite supplied for the American Telephone and Telegraph Company Building in New York City (1979) precipitated a boom for the quarry. In 1996, a new corporate entity— Castellucci Granite Company, LLC, owned by the Boston-based investment firm High Street Group, Inc.—took over the lease.

In late 1999, the Stony Creek quarry was shut down for several months. Meanwhile, the Town of Branford and a managing partner of High Street Group, Inc., completed an amended lease agreement with terms granting more favorable royalties to the town. During the shutdown, Branford First Selectman Anthony DaRos received telephone calls from architects and contractors in such faraway places as Australia, China, and Mexico, as well as in New York State and Texas, asking for his assistance in reopening operations. The amended lease agreement took effect on December 30, 1999, and the granite company's name was changed to Stony Creek Granite Company, LLC. This allowed Stony Creek's "premium" granite to return to the world stone market under its own well-known name. The quarry's reserves will suffice throughout the current century to maintain the prominence of Stony Creek granite in America's building tradition.

—JH

Architecture terms to know

ashlar	a squared stone
balustrade	a low parapet
castellated	in the style of a castle
coping	the covering course of masonry atop a wall
cruciform	in the shape of a cross
denticulated cornice	an overhanging molding formed by block-like projections
dentil	one of a series of small, projecting, rectangular blocks
egg and dart	a carved ornament in relief that alternates an egg-like shape with that of an arrowhead
fenestration	the arrangement of a building's openings (such as doors and windows)
grade	the degree of incline
loggia	a roofed open gallery, typically on an upper story
modillion	an ornamental bracket
pediment	a gable end decoration
pilasters	projecting piers of shallow depth
rusticated (as a building's exterior)	building face of masonry with beveled or shaped edges and in which mortar joints are pronounced
stucco	plaster for exterior walls

146

STONY CREEK PINK AT HOME

Not all of the stone quarried in Branford left the town. Stony Creek pink granite appears in many old foundations, curbstones, front steps, fence posts, and exterior walls. It graces retaining walls, monuments, rock gardens, and even kitchen counters. Its durable beauty made it a favorite in its home town.

Laying of the cornerstone, September 26, 1901, Church of Christ, Stony Creek

CHURCH OF CHRIST

Norcross Brothers donated the granite used for the Church of Christ (1901–1903), located on Stony Creek's own Thimble Islands Road. Fortuitously for the village, an industry strike freed quarry workers to volunteer their expert skills. They cut granite blocks onsite with hand tools and constructed the church's meticulously jointed, random *ashlar* (squared stone).

Branford contractor Benjamin F. Hosley (1852–1917) began work on the Church of Christ in August 1901. On September 26, 1901, the cornerstone was laid, and on July 23, 1903, the sanctuary was dedicated. Designed by New York City architect Ernest S. Greene (1864–1936), the Tudor revival church prominently displays a 40-foot (12-meter) granite belltower with *castellated* battlements (in the style of a castle), which also houses the main entrance. While the lower walls and central bay are also of granite, the remaining walls, now shingled, were

Church of Christ,
Stony Creek

originally *stucco* (plaster for exterior walls).
Inside the *cruciform* (cross-shaped) structure, the
ash finish and spruce beams are accented with
woodwork in a quatrefoil motif that is echoed
outside. Ten stained-glass windows, some
installed at later dates, surround three sides of the
sanctuary. To the sanctuary's rear, and closed off
by sliding pocket doors with leaded-glass
windows, is the original Sunday school room
with its nine stained-glass windows and fireplace.

WILLOUGHBY WALLACE MEMORIAL LIBRARY

Five and a half decades after Stony Creek's
Church of Christ was built, Castellucci & Sons,
Inc., donated large granite blocks for construction
of the Willoughby Wallace Memorial Library
(1958) just up the road from the church. Drill
holes used to blast the rock out of granite ledge
remain visible on the exterior walls.

Having no heirs, Willoughby Adelbert
Wallace (1854–1946) surprised Branford
residents when he bequeathed the bulk of his
estate to the town for construction of a free
public library in Stony Creek. Wallace's sole

business undertaking—a barnlike roller-skating
rink—failed. Nevertheless, his estate surpassed
$90,000. In his will, he stipulated that the town
must accept his bequest within 10 years or the
sum would revert to Stony Creek's Church of
Christ. After considerable debate, Town Meeting
members voted on February 29, 1956, to accept
Wallace's gift.

New Haven architect and Stony Creek
resident Douglas Orr (1892–1966) offered to
design the library building at no cost to the town.
Orr had an affinity for Stony Creek pink granite,
which he described as "an enduring and noble
material because of its lovely texture and color . . .
the kind of [stone] you'd want to put into an
important building." Ground was broken in
October of 1956, and Thornton J. Converse
(1891–1965), also of Stony Creek and a member
of the Orr firm, supervised the building's

Willoughby Wallace Memorial Library, Stony Creek

Isaac C. Lewis Fountain,
Stony Creek

construction. The library opened to the public on November 1, 1958, a distinctive example of the "contemporary" style of the time. In spite of Orr's traditional training in architecture at Yale University and his subsequent European studies at the American Academy in Rome and the École des Beaux Arts, he had readily embraced new architectural trends that prevailed in the 1940s and 1950s. Several of his commissions, including the Wallace Library, were characterized by geometric simplicity, expansive glass windows, flat roofs, and a reliance on the decorative qualities of building materials for esthetic effect. The Castellucci company's $5,000 contribution in granite, made shortly after the company's acquisition of the Stony Creek quarry from the Dodds Granite Company in 1955, not only helped Orr realize his architectural vision, but also assisted in creating a lasting community resource that is much appreciated by its patrons.

ISAAC C. LEWIS FOUNTAIN

Not all monuments were motivated by public remembrance. Private citizens, as well, sought lasting memorials for individuals removed by death from those who knew and loved them. For example, the Isaac C. Lewis Fountain (1917), located on a small triangle of land formed by

Thimble Islands Road and Indian Point Road in Stony Creek, was given by Kate A.L. Chapin (1851–1914) in memory of her father. The fountain commemorates Isaac Chauncy Lewis (1812–1893) as a prominent citizen of Meriden, Connecticut, and an early summer resident of Stony Creek. The monument is constructed of granite ashlar in the shape of a cube. It sits on a graceful base and is capped by a thin slab on which rests a decorative sphere supported by whimsical sea creatures. A large basin, probably used originally for watering animals, projects on the south side, or Indian Point Road side, of the memorial. The design has water falling into the basin from a small, bronze lion's head. A smaller basin, extending from an apse-like recess on the monument's opposite side, serves as a drinking fountain. The Lewis Fountain was fabricated by John Melander (1866–1918), a talented local stonecutter who lived on Watrous Road. The black-speckled, pinkish-tan granite blocks used in the monument are believed to have come from a large boulder found nearby in the vicinity of Three Elms Road.

149

Damascus Cemetery
wall, Branford

DAMASCUS CEMETERY WALL

Although documentation for utilitarian
structures in Branford and Guilford is sparse,
the productivity of quarry workers in both
communities is visible in the widespread use of
local granite for building foundations, bridge
abutments, walls, breakwaters, piers, pavement
blocks, and hitching posts. Notable Branford
examples include the lower walls of the Ablondi
Building (1889) on Leete's Island Road, the
retaining walls at Bayview Park on Thimble
Islands Road, and the Pine Orchard seawall on
Long Island Sound. In 1899, Timothy L. Barker
(1828–1911), a Branford native who settled in
Oakland, California, donated the granite walls
and iron gate that enclose Damascus Cemetery
(established c. 1812), located near the intersection
of Damascus and Totoket Roads in Branford.
The mason, William Olver of New Haven,
completed the handsomely crafted, 3.5-foot

(1.07-meter) walls from rough-faced ashlar
supplied for $700 by Norcross Brothers.
In Guilford, granite was also specified for the
railroad overpass abutments along State
Route 146, for the footings of Jones Bridge
on Water Street, and for the Sachem's Head
Harbor Breakwater.

—JH

STONY CREEK PINK AT LARGE

Stony Creek pink granite gained a sterling reputation for good reason. It was lauded for its "superior quality," praised as "an unusual . . . and artistic material." One buyer went so far as to say: "[W]e know of no granite that can compare with either Stony Creek or Pink Milford granite . . ." As the granite traveled, its reputation grew, until it was recognized not only regionally and nationally, but internationally as well.

NEWBERRY LIBRARY

The Newberry Library in Chicago, Illinois, was completed on November 15, 1893, the final result of a generous bequest by banking and real estate magnate Walter Loomis Newberry (1804–1868). The Braintree Granite Company of Boston, Massachusetts, had originally been chosen by the well-known Chicago architect Henry Ives Cobb (1859–1931) to provide stone for the library. However, delays in delivery and difficulties in cutting the hard granite (known as Dedham granite) forced Cobb to look for another supplier. He then chose Norcross Brothers of Worcester, Massachusetts. After visiting the company's quarries in Branford, Connecticut, and Milford, Massachusetts, Cobb selected Stony Creek pink granite for the remaining stone needed to complete the library. Much to his frustration, further delays ensued in 1892 when the New England Granite Manufacturers Association temporarily suspended operations in affiliated quarries until contractual disputes could be resolved. When library construction resumed, Stony Creek pink was still the stone of choice.

Cobb is believed to have based his design for the Newberry Library on the Marshall Field Warehouse (1885–1887) in Chicago. Plans for this Renaissance revival, palazzo-type block built of rough-faced granite came from influential Boston architect and former École student Henry Hobson Richardson (1838–1886). Cobb's design, a long symmetrical edifice with center and end pavilions, followed a rigidly prescribed program. According to historian Houghton Wetherold:

[I]n the Newberry facade, Cobb modified the Richardsonian aesthetic significantly. Only in the first story did Cobb allow himself Richardson's rugged masonry and deep window reveals in order to create an

151

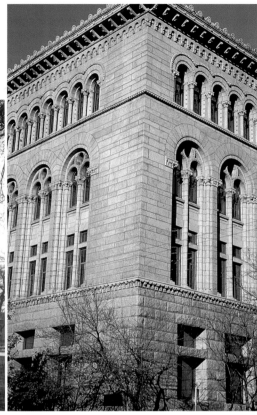

Newberry Library,
Chicago

adequately strong-looking base for the solid walls of the
upper floors. Above the basement story, the wall surface,
built of hard, precise blocks of Braintree [and Stony
Creek] granite, is tough and severe, the edges of the
projecting pavilions sharp and clear. A Richardson
building, wrapped in its warm rough protective shell,
seems to dilate with its contained volume, but the
Newberry, more rigorous, more abstract, bold not from
ruggedness but from its flat severity and density, appears
to breath[e] in rather than out.

CONNECTICUT GENERAL INSURANCE COMPANY BUILDING

Completed in 1926, the former Connecticut
General Insurance Company Building in
Hartford provides the capital city with its most
distinguished example of Renaissance revival
architecture. Its designer, New York City

architect James Gamble Rogers (1867–1947),
was trained at Yale University in New Haven,
Connecticut, and the École des Beaux Arts. He
also designed many of Yale University's
buildings. The General Insurance Company
Building's Stony Creek granite elevations are
based on the Medici-Riccardi Palace in Florence,
Italy. Six stories high, with ten bays on Hudson
Street, seven bays on Elm Street, and a cutaway
corner entrance within a central, two-story arch,
the composition reads as a single massive facade
fronting on Pulaski Circle. The first two stories
are *rusticated*—that is, the mortar joints are
pronounced, with the stones' rounded edges
deeply cut back to about 6 inches (15 cm). On the
first story, Rogers used arched windows faced
with ornate iron grilles. On the upper stories,
the building's *fenestration*—the arrangement

of its openings—is paired and rectangular. *Denticulated cornices,* which are overhanging moldings formed by block-like projections, run above the second and fourth stories, while the building's prominent main cornice has *dentils, egg-and-dart molding,* and large *modillions* (ornamental brackets). This building was fabricated in Providence, Rhode Island, by the Providence Granite Company from Stony Creek granite supplied from the Norcross Brothers Quarry by the Dodds Granite Company.

FULTON BUILDING

Although some buildings were finished in Stony Creek granite, the decorative pink stone was more commonly used as an accent material, often at the base level. The Fulton Building (1905–1906) in Pittsburgh, Pennsylvania, is a 13-story, steel-framed, Renaissance revival skyscraper the lower floors of which are clad with rough-faced granite. The granite contrasts in both tone and texture with the buff-colored brick used above. The former office building features an interior lightwell framed by a magnificent seven-story arch facing Duquesne Boulevard. The arch serves both to structurally bridge the building's top stories and to visually unify the multiple arched elements of the exterior. Currently under rehabilitation as a

Connecticut General Insurance Company Building, Hartford (above)

Fulton Building, Pittsburgh (left)

153

South Station Headhouse,
Boston

hotel, the Fulton Building was designed by
New York City architect Grosvenor Atterbury
(1869–1956). After graduating from Yale
University in 1891, Atterbury attended
Columbia University's School of Architecture
and apprenticed with the prestigious New York
architectural firm of McKim, Mead & White.
He completed his architectural training at the
École des Beaux Arts.

BOSTON'S SOUTH STATION HEADHOUSE

The Boston architectural firm of Shepley, Rutan,
and Coolidge was active in Chicago during and
after the 1893 World's Columbian Exposition in
that city. Its neoclassical revival design for
Boston's South Station Headhouse (1896–1899)
resembles that of the Exposition's Terminal
Station, built from plans by Chicago architect

Grand Central Terminal,
New York City

Charles B. Atwood (1848–1895). Constructed by Norcross Brothers with granite from Stony Creek, South Station remains a major transportation landmark in New England. Five stories in height, the elaborate, classically inspired headhouse curves gracefully along Atlantic Avenue and Summer Street. The focal point of the building is an ornate clock-piece, topped by a monumental stone eagle, presiding above the station's main entrance. In 1986, two wings were added to the main headhouse using the same Stony Creek granite from the Norcross Brothers Quarry.

GRAND CENTRAL TERMINAL

"Modern cities have no portals or arches of triumph," declared New York City architect Whitney Warren (1864–1943). Credited with the

design for his city's Grand Central Terminal (completed in 1913), Warren concluded, "Their real gateways are the railroad stations, and the motive of the facade of this terminal is an attempt to offer a tribute to commerce." The base of Warren's monumental Beaux Arts-style edifice from street level to upper-roadway *balustrade*— a low parapet—is faced with Stony Creek pink granite (the walls above are Bedford limestone). The distinctive stonework that frames the storefronts and lines the covered taxi area of the terminal is visible to pedestrians on 42nd Street and Vanderbilt Avenue. Grand Central took 10 years to build and employed a number of engineers and architects before the concept for the station's complex multilevel plan could be completed. Architect Warren graduated from Columbia University in 1886 and, like most of

155

his contemporaries, studied at the École des Beaux Arts. Upon his return to America after 10 years in Paris, he worked for the firm of McKim, Mead & White in New York City until establishing his own practice with Charles D. Wetmore (1867–1941). A true Francophile, Warren helped found New York's Society of Beaux Arts Architects, and he became both an officer in the Legion d'Honneur and a member of the Institute de France. His training at the École is evident in Grand Central's symmetrical elevations and exuberant ornamentation, including the sculpted group—Mercury, Hercules, and Minerva—by Jules Coutan (1848–1939) that surrounds the great clock on the southern elevation.

AMERICAN TELEPHONE AND TELEGRAPH COMPANY BUILDING

In the two decades following the acquisition of the Dodds Granite Company by Castellucci and Sons, Inc., the quarry's operation was limited by the prevailing architectural preference for glass and concrete buildings. Not until the late 1970s was the use of stone revived, when influential New York City architect Philip Johnson (1906–) chose Stony Creek granite to face the American Telephone and Telegraph Company Building in New York City (1979).

American Telephone and Telegraph Company Building, New York City

"The heat loss from [glass] curtain walls," he explained, "is too great and the price of aluminum has probably more than doubled." Johnson's postmodern skyscraper includes historic references—most noticeably an open recessed Palladian court at street level and a "Chippendale" broken *pediment* (gable end decoration) at the tower's roofline. Subsequently, other prominent architectural firms followed Johnson's lead to build such major stone structures as the Society Tower/Marriott Hotel in Cleveland, Ohio (Cesar Pelli & Associates); Momentum Place in Dallas, Texas (John Burgee Architects); Columbia Square in Washington, D.C. (Pei, Cobb, Freed, and Partners); and 125 Summer Street in Boston, Massachusetts (Kohn Pederson Fox).

STATUE OF LIBERTY NATIONAL MONUMENT

The Statue of Liberty National Monument (1886) was created in copper by French sculptor Frederic Auguste Bartholdi (1834–1904) in honor of America's centennial. It was presented to the people of the United States by the government of France in 1876. The gift did not arrive in New York City until June 17, 1885, however, because of financial difficulties in installing the base at Fort Hood on Bedloe's Island, now known as Liberty Island. Ground was finally broken

Statue of Liberty National Monument, New York Harbor

for the statue's 53-foot (16-meter) granite pedestal in April 1883, and the 6-ton (5.4-tonne) cornerstone was laid on August 5, 1884.

Granite for the base came from Beattie's Quarries at Leete's Island in Guilford, which in 1884 was operating at full tilt. Quarry workers carefully numbered each granite block, then loaded the stone into an ox-drawn sled to be hauled to Hoadley's Point. From there, it could be shipped to New York Harbor along the Connecticut and New York coasts. The celebrated New York City architect Richard Morris Hunt (1828–1895), the first American to study at the École des Beaux Arts, donated his design for the statue's high platform, itself an imposing architectural form. Confronted with the challenge of creating a structure that was both a major focal point and a visual foil for *Liberty,* Hunt designed a boldly scaled, concrete and steel-backed, neoclassical revival pedestal. He faced the pedestal in rusticated and smooth granite with striking neo-Grec detailing. Doorways were surmounted by heavy, unornamented pediments and flanked by smooth *pilasters* (projecting piers of shallow depth) with circular shields. A frieze of 40 shields, symbolizing the 40 states then comprising the Union, encircles the pedestal. Above the structure's shaft, which is treated identically on each side, is a deeply recessed *loggia* (open gallery) set above smooth stone panels originally intended for incised inscriptions; the tapered corner walls are of rusticated granite blocks. An observation platform is set behind the pedestal's parapet and surrounded by bold arched uprights. This vantage point allows a magnificent view of New York Harbor and, skyward, an astonishing glimpse of *Liberty* in all her colossal splendor. The pedestal was completed in time for the statue's dedication on October 28, 1886, thanks to generous contributions from hundreds of citizens. At the time, *Liberty* was the tallest figure (151 feet/46 meters) created by humankind, the largest piece of copper statuary in history, and—as it remains— the world's most renowned symbol of political freedom.

EQUESTRIAN STATUE OF MAJOR GENERAL JOHN SEDGWICK

Stony Creek granite was often specified for the platforms and pedestals of Civil War monuments built throughout the country, and for the most part, it was the Norcross Brothers firm that cut the granite required by the numerous memorials. Notable among these is the bronze Equestrian Statue of Major General John Sedgwick on the Battlefield of Gettysburg in Pennsylvania (1913). In 1909, the Connecticut General Assembly appropriated $25,000 for a memorial to Major General Sedgwick, an honored son from Cornwall and commander of the Sixth Corps, Army of the Potomac, who was killed in battle on May 9, 1864, at Spottsylvania, Virginia. In the sculptor's memorandum of

Equestrian Statue of Major General John Sedgwick, Gettysburg

design to the Major General John Sedgwick Equestrian Statue Commission, H.K. Bush-Brown stated:

As the statue is to be placed on the Battlefield of Gettysburg, I have endeavored to represent General Sedgwick as he might have appeared on his arrival there, overlooking that part of the field which his troops were to occupy. The horse with head erect and his whole expression alert to the situation. The size of the statue to be one and one-half life size. The pedestal to be of polished Stony Creek granite, in two pieces, as shown in the design. The size of the pedestal to be about 12 feet by 6 feet by 5½ feet (3.6 m × 1.8 m × 1.7 m). The pedestal to have a platform 28 feet × 22 feet (8.5 m × 6.7 m), surrounded by a coping of granite on a 3-foot (0.9-meter) foundation. . . .

SOLDIERS MONUMENT

Cities and towns in Connecticut erected Civil War memorials for their own brave men who died in battle. One such tribute, the Soldiers Monument (1877, 1887), is prominently located on the Town Green in Guilford. The designs for the memorial's platform, pedestal, and soldier were based on plans originally prepared by the James G. Batterson Company of Hartford; however, the contract to erect the monument went to John Beattie (1820–1899), whose quarry

Soldiers Monument, Guilford

on Leete's Island produced the tall, pink granite base in 1877. Ten years later, Thomas Phillips & Son of New Haven fabricated the statue in gray granite from Quincy, Massachusetts. The Soldiers Monument was dedicated twice—first on May 30, 1877, when the pedestal was installed, and second on July 2, 1887, when the statue of a Civil War soldier was put in place. Although conventional in concept, the memorial's execution had an unusual history, since it involved two out-of-town firms using granite for a monument base that was provided by a third, local concern.

OLD HARBOR BREAKWATER

The scope and challenge of projects undertaken by Beattie's Quarries are readily evident in the Old Harbor Breakwater (1870–1876) on Block Island, in Rhode Island. Funds for construction were appropriated by the United States Congress

159

in recognition of the potential of the island's township, New Shoreham, as a summer resort. Beattie's Quarries' first granite shipment on the schooner *D.H. Baldwin* was put overboard at Block Island on October 27, 1870. Hundreds of

Old Harbor Breakwater, Block Island

160

oak pilings were driven to an average depth of 7 feet (2.1 m) in order to stabilize the jetties' cribwork. Upon the breakwater's completion, the quarry had supplied approximately 90,000 tons (81,000 t) of riprap at a cost of $155,000. *The New York Times* called the result "one of the most extensive engineering works undertaken of late" in the Northeast.

The Old Harbor Breakwater consists

of two jetties: One, extending approximately 1,500 feet (457 m) from shore in a northeast direction, provides protection for the east side of Old Harbor; the other, a 1,000-foot (305-meter), L-shaped arm extending east, forms the inner harbor itself. Beacons placed at the outer end of each jetty mark the harbor's 300-foot (91.4-meter) wide entrance. At the request of the island's residents, the temporary basin constructed within the harbor for the breakwater's building equipment was left intact. Improvements over the years and the addition of a new ferry landing have only minimally affected the visual integrity of the breakwater that forms Old Harbor and the inner basin.

BULKELEY BRIDGE

On occasion, quarries at Leete's Island and Stony Creek collectively provided granite for large-scale undertakings such as the Bulkeley Bridge (c. 1904–1908) over the Connecticut River. Known as the Hartford Bridge until 1928, this unusually long, stone-arch structure carries two wide roadways for Interstate 84 between Hartford and East Hartford. The elegant, neoclassical revival design was a collaborative effort by chief engineer Edwin D. Graves (1865–c. 1908) and Boston architect Edmund M. Wheelwright (1854–1912). The bridge consists of

Bulkeley Bridge, Hartford

nine semi-elliptical spans set on piers supported by concrete-filled, wooden caissons sunk up to 50 feet (15.2 m) below the river. The base of each pier is finished in rough-faced, gray ashlar from Beattie's Quarries, and the arches, piers, and railing are constructed of Stony Creek pink-gray ashlar supplied by Norcross Brothers. At the time of its completion in 1908, the Bulkeley Bridge was considered a major engineering accomplishment in Connecticut. According to historian Bruce Clouette:

Because of its magnitude, as well as the requirements of deep foundations in the river bed and an immense quantity of precisely cut stone, the Bulkeley Bridge presented great challenges in design, construction, and project management. . . . [It] was the most costly bridge in Connecticut and among the longest stone-arch bridges in the world. Its monumental scale, arched form, graceful geometry, fine stonework, and simple neoclassical ornament were intended to create an

entrance to Hartford that would be worthy of its status as a prosperous commercial and industrial city. To this end, the project cleared out tenement blocks and built wide, tree-lined boulevards at either end. The Bulkeley Bridge is one of the state's foremost outcomes of the early twentieth century "City Beautiful" movement.

—JH

161

THE BATTLE MONUMENT AT WEST POINT

Following the Civil War, Americans' attention turned toward commemorating the men who courageously served during the conflict. Nowhere was this sentiment more movingly expressed than at the Battle Monument of the United States Military Academy at West Point, New York (1897).

The memorial honors 188 officers and 2,042 enlisted men of the Regular Army of the United States who were killed in action or subsequently died of wounds suffered during the "War of the Rebellion." In 1863, a small group of West Point graduates who to that point had survived the war formed a Battle Monument Committee to construct an appropriate memorial. The following year, a persuasive circular was issued to West Point officers suggesting subscription rates based on military rank. By 1865, a total of $14,393.54 had been raised, although sufficient funds to build the monument were not available until 1890.

In evaluating several architects' prospective sketches and design philosophies, the Battle Monument Committee sought expert assistance from architects Richard Morris Hunt and Arthur Rotch (1850–1894), and sculptor Augustus Saint-Gaudens (1848–1907). The committee eventually commissioned McKim, Mead & White to execute the memorial, based on a drawing submitted by

the fashionable and highly gifted New York City architect Stanford White (1853–1906). White envisioned a single granite victory column that would not compete with the extraordinary natural beauty of the site's overlook on the Hudson River. To sculpt the figure of *Fame*, which would top the column, the committee selected Frederick William MacMonnies (1863–1937). Norcross Brothers in Stony Creek, well known for its capacity to produce large stones, was chosen to build the monument.

The fabrication of the shaft for the Battle Monument—46 feet (14 m) high and 96 tons (86.4 t)—was considered a major engineering triumph for the Norcross company. At the time of its completion, the polished, rose-colored granite column was believed to be the largest in the world. Norcross undertook the just as impressive challenge of transporting the column to West Point in a 30-ton (27-tonne) wooden crate carried on two flatbed railroad cars. The 191-mile (307-kilometer) trip took nearly two

weeks to complete (38 hours in actual running time). After the preliminary railroad journey to Fishkill, New York, the shaft was transferred in its crate to a boat for shipment to Newburgh. Upon landing in Newburgh, the column needed once again to travel overland, this time up the Military Academy's steep hill to the monument's magnificent site. This leg alone took another five weeks. An engine-powered windlass winched 126 tons (113.4 t) of crate and column along temporary railroad tracks laid from West Point Station to Trophy Point—tracks that were laid piece by piece at the forward end of the train, while the back end was dismantled to be moved ahead. Once its burden was in place, the same engine hoisted the crated column to an upright position. A neoclassical revival capstone was installed next, followed by a granite sphere surmounted by a bronze figure. For the memorial's low, circular platform, capstone,

and decorative spheres, Norcross Brothers used contrasting black-speckled pink granite quarried at its Milford, Massachusetts, operation.

Upon viewing the completed work, which had been scheduled for dedication in November 1894, Stanford White judged the bronze statue

163

Battle Monument at West Point

164

awkwardly composed and its proportions totally out of scale with the monument. Because MacMonnies's work conformed to the figure depicted by White in his original presentation drawing, McKim, Mead & White agreed to absorb the cost of having the statue redesigned and replaced by the sculptor, which necessitated the postponement of the Battle Monument's dedication until May 31, 1897.

At the dedication, Lieutenant General John M. Schofield, then Chief of Staff of the United States Army, concluded the ceremony with the following remarks:

It is altogether well and worthy that these names of enlisted men are borne upon this monument in one grand muster roll with those of their commanders. Could this shaft, now towering above us, have been built as high as the deeds of the men in whose memory it is erected deserve, its capstone, indeed, would be lost beyond the skies.

—JH

CHANGING TIMES

SOCIAL REFORM

At the same time that the granite industry struggled with antagonisms from within, social pressures from without added to the tension. The growing national temperance movement took a huge step toward Prohibition when the Anti-Saloon League was founded in 1893. The Anti-Saloon League convinced many large industries to contribute significant sums of money to finance the national crusade for temperance and to prohibit the use of liquor by employees. Drunkenness affected not only productivity but safety, League promoters explained. After the successful enlistment of the railroads, many other industries followed suit. Industrialists and business owners used their businesses to advance the temperance cause, enacting prohibitions of alcohol not only on the job but in the privacy of workers' homes. In return, they were lauded for their moral stance, as well as their shrewd business practice.

Senator William J. Clark (1825–1909) of Southington and Stony Creek had acted on the issue of temperance early on. He was even credited with shutting down the saloons in Southington. A prominent manufacturer, businessman, and politician, he owned and operated a factory that made nuts and bolts, and—during the Civil War—gun screws. Active in Republican politics all his life, he served as a state Senator beginning in 1882, chairing a committee on claims, temperance, and Constitutional amendments. One of the

THE LUNDQUIST HOUSE
Mrs. Lundquist had the greenest thumb in town.

early cottagers who built his beautiful "cottage" at the top of Prospect Hill, he became active in Stony Creek affairs. Although never a member of any church, he was a Stony Creek Church trustee and instrumental in seeing that the present church edifice, lavish for its time and culture, was built properly.

Senator Clark believed strongly in temperance. In business practices typical of the era, he did not allow any of his factory employees to drink, even at home. "Mr. Clark also followed closely in his father's footsteps, in regard to the

167

temperance movement," states the *New Haven Annals,* "so much so that no saloons could be run successfully in the neighborhood of the factory." The writer continues:

It was a fundamental principle of Mr. Clark to give preference to employees who did not use intoxicating beverages, and who faithfully devoted their earnings to the proper support of those dependent upon them, believing the economic question and the danger of having powerful machinery run by men with brain and nerves disordered by the use of alcohol, sufficient for the rule. The result was that two saloons existing in that district in 1851 soon retired or moved out and it became a sufficient recommendation to any other factories in the town for an employee seeking a position to quote that he had fulfilled a year at the Clark shop. Throughout his life all beneficial and reform measures that made for the good and rights of people have ever found in Mr. Clark a vigilant and hearty champion.

In his funeral sermon, preached in the Stony Creek Church in 1909, the Rev. E.S. Holloway of Hartford declared: ". . . [T]hrough his whole life he has been rooting up the evils that he found everywhere. . . . [I]n that heart I believe, and ever will, that there was a love of Christ and a faith in Christ that found expression through his active, busy life, and that opened before him at last the

gates of day." One of the church's stained-glass windows, depicting the 12-year-old Jesus with the inscription above, "Great peace have they who love thy law," (Psalms 119:165), seems a fitting tribute to the fruitful life of a stalwart character.

Yet Stony Creek had its ups and downs around the issue of "intoxicating drink." Certainly, when building lots on Money and Governor's Islands were being advertised for sale in the late 1860s, the 1869 *Attractions of New Haven, Connecticut* touted the islands as good for those "seeking piety, temperance, and the domestic order of the home," all typical Protestant values of the time.

Yet there were those who told a different tale. The Rev. Elijah C. Baldwin, who wrote the first history of Stony Creek in 1879, was an ardent prohibitionist. His sympathies no doubt color his history:

Previous to the opening of the Shore line railroad in 1852, Stony Creek had but four houses and but few residences. It was considerably visited by farmers and others from the back country at certain seasons. These generally came in companies and camped out in wagons, or barns, or sheds, mostly at night. They came to "rough it" for a few days. Some of them were at times "rough" in their behavior because of liquor which they brought with them or found in some little stores and "saloons" by the shore. The natives gave them the name of "Portuguese." Stony Creek under such patronage had somewhat of an ill name.

Reverend Baldwin served as the pastor of the Branford Congregational Church from 1865 until 1878, when he was forced out of his pastorate. In the four years before he was appointed to another pastorate in Cheshire, Baldwin wrote extensively for the New Haven Historical Society on the early history of Branford and produced his own magazine called *The Home World.* He had close ties to Stony Creek because of his work in the formation of the Union Religious Society, the building of Union Chapel, and the gathering of the Stony Creek Congregational Church.

At first, Baldwin was a popular minister in Branford, but things went awry over a building expansion project, declining attendance, and ebbing financial support. Certainly, Baldwin's abrasive personality did not help him. In a lengthy, contentious process, he was forced out of ministerial office in 1878 by a decision of the New Haven East Consociation, a regional association of Congregational churches. Nowhere do records directly say that he was forced out because of temperance sermonizing, but they imply that it was involved. Rupert Simons writes:

Mr. Baldwin aspired to be a reformer. He saw much evil about him and felt called upon to correct it. Especially did he set his face against the saloons, and not without need, for there were only forty-two place[s] in town, at that time, where liquor was sold. The parsonage was directly across from one of these "rum holes" and it needed no super-intellect to discern the terrible fruits of its influence upon the community, especially upon the young men. So the minister's sermons were not over tame, despite their bookish idiom, and people came out in large numbers, and enjoyed his invectives—for a while.

The passing years had made for Elijah C. Baldwin not a few enemies and had alienated from him some firm friends. His efforts toward reformation, which at first had been warmly seconded and had brought him popularity began to arouse criticism and then hostility. Mr. Baldwin was neither a statesman nor a diplomat. He was just a good man with a great zeal for the Kingdom of God and an undiscriminating hatred of evil in all places. He had a somewhat tactless tongue and used it in a way which stung, though it was intended to cure.

Baldwin seems to commend certain people on the basis of their temperance views. Of Henry Frisbie, a leading fisherman and oysterman in

Stony Creek, he wrote: "He is a man of the strictest temperance principles and practice." Of Richard Paine, an engraver who moved to Stony Creek from Springfield, Massachusetts: "He introduced somewhat of Massachusetts ideas of reform and progress." That would have included temperance. Perhaps Baldwin was optimistically shaping, as well as recording, the early history of the burgeoning community. He gloated: "With but few exceptions, the people repudiated liquor as ruinous to the welfare of any community. Industry and thrift are manifest on every hand."

Temperance was actively championed in Stony Creek's Protestant pulpit, as well, in keeping with trends across the land. Frank Smith, respected owner of the thriving Stony Creek Oyster Company and a church deacon for almost 60 years, from 1891 to 1949, preached a sermon in January 1900 entitled, "The Sin of Liquor Selling: Why It Must Stop." An election may have been underway. Towns voted annually in local initiative elections.

Dr. Theophilus Devitt, pastor of the Branford Congregational Church from 1893 to 1909, is credited with shutting down the saloons in Branford. He preached a series of sermons entitled "The Evil of Liquor." The town voted itself "dry" in 1908 for the first time in 16 years by a 438 to 376 vote. Branford seldom voted dry,

and the following year, the vote back to wet was one of the highest votes ever recorded, 502 to 349. After 1899, the town of Branford voted by districts. Between 1899 and 1905, Stony Creek voted to prohibit liquor. After 1905, except in 1911, it voted "wet." Guilford almost always voted itself dry.

In the 1880s and 1890s, Stony Creek had tended to be dry, having a greater reputation for temperance than next-door Branford. "For many years the intemperance of so many of the people has been a drawback to Branford," wrote Elijah Baldwin in his magazine, *The Home World.* "A local pride is shown" in Stony Creek "which is commendable and which might be profitably emulated by the citizens of other portions of Branford. With but few exceptions the people repudiate liquor selling as ruinous to the welfare of any community." In the years 1877 to 1917, Branford voted overwhelmingly, often by more than two-to-one margins, to allow the sale of liquor.

A *New Haven Evening Register* article in 1892 notes that in Stony Creek, "There is no liquor sold in the town and what does come there comes to private families and is not delivered in the streets in the shape of unseemly enthusiasm." In 1899, the *Branford Opinion* reported, "Its attractiveness is increased by the fact that Stony

Creek allows no places for the sale of liquor or intoxicating drink." Nevertheless, after the turn of the century, Stony Creek gained an unseemly reputation because of the saloons and drinking that came to proliferate.

It is said that an ardent Pine Orchard temperance leader once bought several acres of Stony Creek salt marsh, south of Buena Vista Road, and divided the land—called Ozone Park in 1909—into very small parcels for sale to other temperance supporters. This gave them voting privileges in order to try to vote the village dry in district elections. Many deeds to homes on Prospect Hill still have temperance restrictions prohibiting the sale of liquor on the premises.

Because Guilford commonly voted dry, Guilford workers, especially quarry workers, would flood into Stony Creek on weekends to go to the many saloons to get drunk. This is how Linda Trowbridge Baxter described it:

The life of the quarry workers was hard, and there was very little time or energy left for recreation. Still, the life of these immigrants offered some diversions and pleasures. For some quarry workers, drinking was an important social activity and outlet after a day's work. . . . [T]hey didn't drink hard liquor the way the Yankees did, but ships from Stony Creek bearing casks of beer and red wine were frequently unloaded at the

LaVassa Colombo Bar

quarry docks. The Guilford Constabulary sometimes pounced on a boatload of beer! During most of the years of the quarry's operation, Guilford was legally a dry town, and while the trolley was in service, every evening but Sunday saw carloads of quarrymen heading for Stony Creek to frequent one of the 7 or 8 saloons there. Carl Balestracci recalls that when he was growing up in Stony Creek, his mother insisted that he remain inside during what is today called the "happy hour!"

A newspaper article after the 1913 election states: "This village was continued in the wet column at Monday's election by a vote of 92 yes and 80 no and the winter patronage from Guilford will continue to keep busy the motormen on the trolley and the barmen at the booze foundries."

171

Folklore and legend abound as people tell and retell stories. "Some of the people who came with the quarries were a floater group, who loved a fight as well as liquor. Seven taverns were doing a thriving business at one time, and the nearby Shoreline towns were dry. Some of their inhabitants were also dry, and on a Saturday night they flooded into Stony Creek, via the old Shore Line trolley, where all could quench their thirst." Numerous anecdotal reports confirm the same. It is said that quarry workers who missed the last trolley back to Guilford could be seen sleeping it off in the bushes on Sunday mornings as people walked to church.

Edith Lake DeLucia, in her reminiscences of growing up in one of the quarry-owned houses, recalls workers amusing themselves by carving granite balls and steps and chiseling designs and names in their time off. She notes: "It was very common for the quarrymen on Sunday—the more simple minded ones—those that didn't go and get drunk—to sit there and carve."

Owen Berio's history of the quarry reports heavy drinking: "The quarry workers were rough and as hard as the stone they worked with. Some were good family men; others unfortunately were not. Liquor of all kinds could be bought at any time." During Prohibition, Leete's Island was noted for its sizable rum-running operation, as were some of the Thimble Islands. In 1925, the large New York vessel *Elizabeth Wilson* was seized at anchor between Little and Big Curtiss Islands by Federal agents. Aboard, the agents discovered 600 cases of hard liquor and a four-man crew.

Temperance had become a grand crusade long before the arrival of the quarry workers. Alcohol abuse did not originate with the immigrants, even if they developed a reputation for heavy drinking. Americans also liked their share, and despite the condemnation leveled by Protestant churches, not all Protestants refrained from drink. However, active members of Protestant

Trolley terminal in Stony Creek

A quarry workers' outing

churches in the late nineteenth century—the pious, professing ones, at least—did not generally drink. And the contrast between them and the drinking, migrant quarry workers could only accentuate whatever divide existed.

Temperance did not travel alone. It was married, for better and worse, to feminism, immigration, Catholicism, social upheaval, and the politics of the labor movement. There was destruction. There was hysteria. There was cruelty. The screams came loud, bold, and raw, echoing even into the hamlets of the land. It was a time when the issues really mattered. So did bread and butter and booze. Roots and freedom and faith mattered, too, as did gold and literacy. And these many matters of heart, politics, and neighborhood so entangled that no one could say where one began and another left off. Even busy little places like Stony Creek knew what was going on. Breaking up the granite rocks of hate, block by block, blast by blast, piece by piece, took time. Destruction of evil took many small chops. It still does.

—WJ

173

The war on John Barleycorn

It is difficult to calculate the impact of the temperance movement on American life. Directed against drinking Protestants, as well as Catholics, the Protestant temperance crusades portrayed the drinking of hard liquor—and increasingly, beer and wine—as "mortal sin." Temperance leaders gradually came to link themselves with other progressive reform movements that focused on the rights of workers, women, and the poor. The interaction was a powerful one.

Before the nineteenth century, Protestants generally viewed alcohol as a good gift of God and taverns as places of beneficent conviviality and community. The use of alcohol at ordinations, dedications, and church functions was common and paid for from church treasuries. Ministers commonly drank, and some even ran stills. At the turn of the eighteenth century, an overabundance of corn led to increased production of distilled liquor, and whiskey consumption surpassed that of rum. The consumption of hard liquor in some regions was exceeding 2 gallons (7.6 l) a year for each adult male.

In the nineteenth century, saloons came to be viewed as a "whore-making, criminal-making, madman-making business." The Second Great Awakening, with its moralistic and theological perfectionism may account for some of the change in attitudes. So, too, may the waves of immigrants with their "excesses," poverty, and public squalor. In any case, saloons stood indicted as destructive of family life, factory discipline, personal morality, and societal stability.

Toward the end of his administration (1801–1809), Thomas Jefferson complained:

The habit of using ardent spirits by men in public office has often produced more injury to the public service, and more trouble to me, than any other circumstance that has occurred in the internal concerns of the country during my administration. And were I to commence my administration again, with the knowledge which from experience I have acquired, the first question that I would ask with regard to every candidate for office should be, "Is he addicted to the use of ardent spirits?"

Presidents Andrew Jackson and Abraham Lincoln echoed Jefferson's concerns about the dangers inherent in the use of alcohol.

Adding fuel to the growing national concern was the known link between drinking, saloons, and prostitution. Yet the saloons were a poor man's social outlet.

The rich man had his club, the middle-class man had his fraternal order, but the poor man had his saloon. Often it was the one bright, cheerful spot in a blighted neighborhood, and "Ladies Not Invited" was a sign frequently seen there. Rather than spend precious leisure in cramped quarters with squalling children and a complaining wife, many men preferred the solace of a saloon, where they could be with friends and enjoy a few hours of fleeting pleasure.

Perry Prann gives a less despairing view of bars in Branford at the turn of the century:

It was often customary for the working man to drop in at his favorite saloon for a drink on his way home from work; not however that the sale of drinks was limited to the workingman, or his after-work hours. The saloon induced a certain camaraderie found nowhere else. Approaching the turn of the century, however, drunkenness on the street was becoming much too frequent, and the saloon came to be regarded by many as a menace. The Women's Christian Temperance Union posed a crusade against it.

The war on saloons intensified with the women's crusades toward the end of the century. The first temperance organization was established in Saratoga, New York, in 1808, followed soon after by ones in Massachusetts and Connecticut in 1813. The first national organization, called the American Society for the Promotion of Temperance, was organized in Boston by two influential Congregational ministers, the Rev. Lyman Beecher—whose "Six Sermons" on the subject were printed and widely circulated—and the Rev. Justin Edwards. By 1833, 6,000 local societies had been organized in several states with more than a million members. Temperance became respectable, promoted even through theater, traveling musical troupes, and popular songs.

Early efforts focused on moral persuasion, encouraging individuals to make voluntary pledges to abstain. Pledgers signed cards or books, promising to "abstain from the use of all intoxicating liquors as a beverage." Some pledges made qualifications: "except for medicinal ➢

The war on John Barleycorn *(continued)*

purposes and religious ordinances." It was in this period that most Protestant churches changed from using wine in communion to using grape juice. After heated lectures and sermons, leaders in a temperance gathering would call for the pledge. The moderates who planned to use alcohol for medicinal or church purposes simply signed. Those declaring "total abstinence" placed a capital T by their names. "Teetotaler" entered the vernacular through this practice.

Henry Frisbie, a leading Stony Creek oysterman and fisherman, refused to use alcohol even for medicinal purposes.

He is a man of the strictest temperance principles and practice. Some years ago he got a terrible wound by the premature discharge of a gun. His limb was nearly blown off. As he lay with wonderful nerve and pluck, the various surgical operations called for, he declared against the belief of his friends, that he should set well, for "I have never touched either tobacco or rum."

Temperance efforts expanded to include the nation's youth. "The Cold Water Army," a children's group organized in 1836 by Presbyterian Rev. Thomas Hunt contended

that prevention is better than cure. Hunt said that if he had 100 drunks to reform, he would be lucky to save 10. If he had 100 children to teach temperance from a young age, he could save 90 of them. Young people were sent out to gather pledges. Education versus later rescue was hotly debated. As in today's antidrug rhetoric, sellers became the evil enslavers of unwitting users.

The Band of Hope, a temperance youth organization founded in England in 1847, spread to the United States. By 1898, a Band of Hope was meeting at the Stony Creek Congregational Church. Catholic temperance organizations for youth developed, even in Branford. Records show an active St. Mary's Total Abstinence and Beneficial Society in 1892, in addition to at least two others for Protestant youth.

No organization so successfully popularized temperance as did the Women's Christian Temperance Union. Organized in 1874, in Cleveland, Ohio, after a year of dramatic protests of marching women, its influence spread rapidly. Soon virtually all Protestant churches, large and small, in cities and small towns across the country, hosted a chapter. The Stony Creek

WCTU was formed in 1888–1889 within the Congregational Church. It met regularly and routinely sent delegates to regional and state rallies.

Politically, the drive for national prohibition began in earnest with the formation of the Anti-Saloon League in 1893 in Ohio. By 1895, it was powered into a national movement by Methodist minister Alpha Kynett, attracting a coalition of several temperance groups that included the WCTU. Voluntary persuasion and pledge-taking no longer sufficed—the demon drink required tough laws that prohibited alcohol uniformly.

The Anti-Saloon League claimed responsibility for the eventual passage in 1919 of the 18th Amendment and the enabling Volsted Act, which created strict laws for the enforcement of national prohibition in 1920. While prohibition laws had already been passed in 33 states, covering close to 65 percent of the population, enforcement was assigned to the Federal government.

In its New Year's greeting in 1920, the League said, "At one minute past twelve tomorrow morning a new nation will be born. . . . Tonight John Barleycorn makes his last will and testament. Now for an era of clear thinking and clean living! The Anti-Saloon League wishes every man, woman and child a happy Dry Year." Sadly, the subsequent 12 years of Prohibition would turn into unmitigated disaster, leading to flagrant lawlessness, bootlegging, physical maiming, gangsterism, and a massive, covert, illegal business.

—WJ

THE DECLINE OF THE GRANITE INDUSTRY

Before the quarries came, Stony Creek could hardly even be described as a village. It had no churches. It had no stores. Who could have guessed the impact the granite industry was about to have? Stony Creek was little more than a few rutted dirt roads—one, today's Route 146, winding along the shore between Guilford and Branford, and others leading north, past scattered farms and cleared fields, to the Post Road. Along the harbor, there were small wharves and fishermen's shacks, from which saltwater farmers put off in their sloops to carry their merchantable crops (including firewood and hay) to Long Island or New Haven, or in rowboats to take oysters, lobsters, or whatever the sea would yield.

New London (and later New Haven) stonecutter B.N. Green's small quarry on Hall's Point was not the only sign that Stony Creek was on the edge of sweeping change in the 1850s. In 1848, surveyors passed through the village, planning the route for a railroad intended to connect New Haven and New London. Two years later, gangs of laborers passed through, grading the roadbed and laying ties and rails. In 1852, the trains began running—opening sleepy little Stony Creek and other hamlets along the shore to the great world.

"Rusticators"—summer vacationers—had been visiting the islands and picturesque coves along the East Shore since as early as the 1830s, when a hotel was built for their accommodation at Sachem's Head. Not until after the completion of the New Haven & New London Railroad, however, did they begin to come in considerable numbers. To meet the increasing demand, the old hotel in Sachem's Head was rebuilt and expanded in 1860. When completed, it boasted a hundred bedrooms, a billiard room, and tenpin alleys, and claimed to be "the largest summer hotel between New York and Newport." Smaller hotels and genteel boardinghouses appeared in Stony Creek by the 1860s. By the 1870s, well-to-do families began building cottages on the Thimble Islands. These developments not only provided employment for natives, but attracted energetic and entrepreneurial men and women who saw opportunities in serving the needs of summer visitors.

The opulent leisure of the summer people must have presented an odd contrast to the grinding labor and poverty of growing numbers of stoneworkers who were flocking to newly opened quarries in Sachem's Head, Leete's Island, and Stony Creek in the 1870s and 1880s. Along with the dramatic growth of quarrying and resort businesses, fishing and oystering—long mainstays of the rural economy—were undergoing dramatic changes. As early as the 1770s, intensive harvesting of oysters had largely depleted stocks of this valuable shellfish. In response, Branford and other shoreline towns passed ordinances limiting the seasons in which oysters could be taken and the amounts oystermen were permitted to harvest. Before the availability of ice (ice harvesting became a significant local industry by the 1830s) and the completion of the railroad, most oysters were taken for local consumption. When these innovations opened a national market for shellfish, clever Yankees devised ways of increasing yields. In the 1860s, a group of entrepreneurs began systematically "seeding" oysterbeds and marketing their crops to seafood wholesalers in New York and Boston. By 1890, the business was largely concentrated in the hands of a handful of firms— chiefly the Stony Creek Oyster Company, organized in 1868.

Stony Creek House
(below, left)

NORCROSS BROTHERS
QUARRY WORKERS
(below, right) The man in the dark suit is probably one of the Norcross Brothers. The youngsters may be tool boys.

The economic transformation of Stony Creek necessarily brought with it a host of improvements in the village's quality of life—school, chapel, fraternal societies. The village's population had grown sufficiently to support its own church congregation and mission services for immigrant worshippers.

The resolutely Yankee pedigrees of Stony Creek's farmers, storekeepers, oystermen, and summer folk and their assorted retainers and caretakers contrasted with the increasingly polyglot character of the quarries' workforce. Some workers lived with their families, but most were single men—often drifters—who lived in dormitories and bunkhouses.

Quarrymen's families lived under the most primitive conditions, as Joel Helander's interview with 91-year-old Narcissa Tonelli, whose parents had come to the Sachem's Head Quarry in 1908, suggests:

A three-room shanty at the main quarry pit became their home. The bedbugs swarmed so badly the first night that they overhauled and disinfected the place. Chairs were lacking, so Gus Tonelli set up empty dynamite kegs.... There were no outhouses on the premises. Mrs. Tonelli drove tree limbs into a hole and lined it with feed bags sewn together. Another hold under the shanty kept their meats and vegetables cool. Workmen blasted two or three times daily. Before each detonation, a man ran through the rows of shanties shouting, "Fire! Fire! Get out of the house!" There was a scramble to safer distances, and according to Mrs. Tonelli, stones came out of the sky "like rain...." Falling debris frequently pelted the roofs of the workmen's barracks. Rain seeped through the ceiling cracks. Mr. Tonelli had an answer for that. He plugged the leaks with tomato can lids, uncleaned, so the residue of tomato paste would make them stick. Someone was injured nearly every day at the Sachem's Head quarry. "A lot of crushed fingers," says Mrs. Tonelli. A whistle on a compressor blasted three times when there was an accident. It signaled a Stony Creek doctor. The quarry laborers worked ten hours a day for six days a week, receiving pay that averaged $1.25 to $1.75 per day, depending on their skills.

It seems unlikely that such improvements as the church and school benefited many quarry workers. Joel Helander's account of the Sachem's Head Quarry mentions that a number of specially favored immigrant workers were provided with jobs that kept them on payrolls during the winter and spring months when the quarry was inactive. But the vast majority moved on to other places. Like other migrant workers, even in our own time, the rank-and-file of quarrymen lived beneath the notice of their betters.

Still, as grim as the quarrymen's life seems to

have been, they found time to worship. They attended mission services conducted by Guilford's Roman Catholic, and Branford's Episcopal, Baptist, and Congregational churches, and visited the now-vanished Swedish Lutheran Church in "Swedesville" on Leete's Island Road, near the railroad tracks that led to the Norcross Brothers (later Castellucci) Quarry. By the 1920s, those who had detached themselves from the stoneworkers' subculture were assimilating into Branford's melting pot.

Even so, the growing gap between the "haves" in their island cottages and the "have-nots" in shanties and bunkhouses by the edges of the quarries might have widened still further had not World War I reshuffled the American economy and economic relations within it. Labor, once absurdly plentiful, became scarce. Men went off to war, and the flow of immigration was curtailed. At the same time, intensive efforts to "Americanize" immigrants—to teach them language and citizenship skills—brought the benefits of literacy to the children of industrial workers and, in many cases, to the workers themselves. The booming economy of the 1920s opened further opportunities: Once unskilled laborers became small businessmen, clerks, and skilled craftsmen—the backbone of the American middle class.

Meanwhile, reinforced concrete had been widely experimented with in the last quarter of the nineteenth century. By 1910, it had become a staple in industrial structures—the New Haven Gas Company's coal bunkers, the New Haven Water Company's Whitneyville Slow Sand Filter, and the New Haven Railroad's Cos Cob electrical generating plant—and so, too, in residential and commercial construction. Within the decade, leading quarries had dramatically reduced their workforces, and many others had shut down entirely. Some faded away. Others, like Maine's Hurricane Island quarry, shut abruptly. "Cement was replacing granite in foundation work," wrote island historians Charles and Carol McLane:

[T]he ornamental stonework of the 1870s and 1880s was going out of vogue, and railroads everywhere were replacing sailing or steam vessels as the transport of choice, which favored the quarries near Barre, Vermont. The Hurricane company was reorganized and limped along until 1914, when two events within a fortnight signaled the end: the sinking of a scow with Hurricane granite in Rockland Harbor during a September gale (an episode hardly unknown in the trade, but disheartening at this particular juncture) and the premature death from typhoid fever of the energetic young superintendent....

OBELISK IN THE QUARRY
This monument now stands in Sault Sainte Marie, Michigan.

When the announcement came one summer's day in 1915 that the quarry was going to be closed, a kind of panic ensued among the quarrymen, stonecutters, blacksmiths, paving cutters, tool sharpeners, tool boys, lumpers, stone boxers, and teamsters and their families. They were given only short notice to pack for the last boat. Many of them were forced to leave some of their possessions behind, and most never returned. The houses were taken down and sold wharfside; the church pews, organ, and altar went to the North Haven Catholic Church, and what remained was floated across Hurricane Sound to Vinalhaven.

Stony Creek quarrymen were spared the trauma of the Hurricane Islanders. Located not only on the mainland but in the midst of a booming and diversified industrial economy, the men and their families did not necessarily have to move elsewhere when the quarry work slowed or ceased. Branford, an industrial suburb, offered jobs at the giant Malleable Iron Fittings Company complex and at the Yale & Towne Manufacturing Company, among others. New Haven, Hartford, Bridgeport, and other manufacturing centers beckoned with opportunities for all men willing to work. Some families stayed; most left, often migrating to still prosperous quarries in Massachusetts (Quincy),

Vermont (Barre), or Maine (Crotch Island and Mount Waldo).

Though seldom successful, strikes, lockouts, and sabotage were common. So were rage and despair, judging from the rising levels of drunkenness and violence between quarry workers by the turn of the century. Some workers, particularly those for whom mastering English was difficult, found themselves trapped in working poverty. Others, at enormous sacrifice, strove to get out of the quarries (although not necessarily out of the industry) by starting small businesses—boardinghouses and grocery stores—which catered to the needs of quarry workers. Still others became quarry owners themselves: By the turn of the century, the advertising sections of industry trade journals were filled with family names that a decade or two earlier had been inscribed on quarry pay and union dues ledgers.

In the old style quarries of the pre-World War I years, human and animal muscle power were joined with simple engineering that used ropes and timbers to extract and finish huge pieces of stone. The triumphant attitudes seen in the surviving photographs of the workers, lined up in front of huge columns or dwarfed by towering wooden cranes, conceal the harshness, danger, and brutality of the quarryman's life.

Occasionally, men were killed or maimed by explosions, falls, or crushing injuries. More often, they fell victim to occupational diseases.

The decline of quarrying, the willingness of some quarrymen to abandon lives of danger and rootlessness, and the passage of time have largely erased the class and ethnic divisions that once characterized Stony Creek. It helped that Branford was a blue-collar town. The sons and daughters of Yankees and those of Italian, Irish, Scots, Swedish, Finnish, Cornish, and English quarry workers went to school together,

worshipped together, fought wars together, and worked side-by-side at MIF, the lockworks, or on the railroad (the region's largest employers). A DaRos (who came in the time of the quarries) is as readily identified today as a "true Creeker" as would be a Brainerd or Paine (whose families came during the 1850s), or a Howd (whose ancestors have been here since the eighteenth century).

Nature has the capacity, within a century, to heal a wounded landscape. It can transform the devastated barrens left by intensive quarrying into forests and wetlands, leaving tracings of the past in the forms of railroad ties rotting in the middle of a nature trail or a huge finished granite architectural element in a stand of wood. So, too, society, with the passage of time, heals the injuries of oppression and exploitation with nostalgia and selective memory.

—PDH

A man and his rock

TORCH AND LOADER

Squeezed between falling market prices and rising labor cost demands, quarries across New England began to fold. When World War I drove the cost of black powder from two dollars a keg to thirteen, there was no returning to what the quarries had been. By 1920, only one quarry, the Norcross, was still in operation in Stony Creek—and at a level less than half of what it had been at its peak.

If the quarry business was to revive, it would need to find a whole new way to bring granite to the marketplace. And after languishing for the first half of the twentieth century a new, post-industrial means of quarrying began to take shape.

It is our mastery over fire—the elemental force we first sought to harness in primeval times—that has most helped us to become modern. As the Stony Creek quarries rose to their peak of activity at the end of the nineteenth century, Nikolaus Otto's internal combustion engine underwent development and Rudolf Diesel invented the engine that bears his name. And in the twentieth century, as Stony Creek granite progressed from primarily structural uses to its popularity as ever thinner slabs of building veneer, the internal combustion engine gave rise to two even more powerful combustion engines—first the jet and then the rocket.

This jet and rocket technology ultimately came to the quarries in the form of a Jet Piercing or Jet Channeling Torch used in the battle of bone against stone. Jet channeling cuts out huge blocks, which are then split into smaller pieces and sent from Stony Creek to places as close as Providence or as far away as Italy for fabricating and finishing.

THE FIRST CUT

The first Jet Channeling Torches used liquid oxygen and burned at a temperature close to 5,000 degrees Fahrenheit (2,760°C). A later model, using compressed air and number two fuel oil, burned at a temperature closer to 3,000 degrees (1,650°C) and was easier to operate. Water runs continuously for this equipment to wash out the debris, keep the nozzle cool, and reduce the dangers of dust. The torch can cut a 2- to 8-inch (5.1- to 20.3-centimeter) channel 20 feet (6.1 m) deep. Because the torches are very

noisy, workers wear earplugs. They do not
generally wear any protection against the
machinery's exhaust fumes.

The stonecutter uses the torch in the
extraction process by cutting the four vertical
sides that define the intended block, leaving
the bottom still connected to the ledge. The
worker then drills a hole into the center of the
bottom plane of the block using a pneumatic
jack drill, after which he rams about 5 pounds
(2.3 kg) of black powder into the hole and
detonates it. The blast lifts the 20 × 30 × 18-foot
(6.1 × 9.1 × 5.5-meter) block a few inches, freeing
it from the ledge gently enough to keep it intact.

Fewer holes and less powder are needed to
free a block along its horizontal plane because
the stone's rift (horizontal proclivity) is more
yielding than its grain (vertical proclivity).
As Steve Castellucci puts it, when it comes to
splitting stone, "There's an easy way, a second
way, and a hard way." The easy way is with the
rift. The second way is with the grain. The hard
way is across the grain, or what is known as
"with the head grain."

Bits for the drills are now made from
carbide steel and can effectively drill about five
times farther than earlier bits before needing
sharpening. They have a total life of about
350 feet (106.7 m).

MOVEABLE STONE

Having freed an enormous block of stone,
the quarry workers are then ready to cut it apart.
Three-foot (0.9-meter) deep holes are drilled
every 8 to 12 inches (20.3 to 30.5 cm) in a line
across the block. Into each hole is put a wedge
and a pair of steel half-rounds—the descendants
of the plugs and feathers. A stonecutter drives
the wedges with a pneumatic hammer—or
by hand—until the block splits. Johnny Barnes
explains the process:

You'd put these three-foot-long [0.9-meter-long]
tapered wedges in a line of holes with half-rounds on
either side, and you tighten with a sledgehammer.

Drilling the stone

As the pressure increased—it was kind of an art—
you tightened the wedges. You couldn't tighten them
too tight, and you had to wait for the crack. You want
the crack to go straight. If you use too much force, it
would run out. It would strike a horizontal and go
down on the 45 and ruin the stone. So as the crack
developed, you had to rest the stone—and also rest the
workers at the same time.

The workers repeat this process until they
have created blocks that weigh about 18 tons
(16.2 t) each—a heft that can reasonably be
put on a truck.

The Norcross, now Castellucci, Quarry at
one point boasted the largest wood derrick—
127 feet (38.7 m) tall. No derricks exist now.
Instead, front-end loaders are used to lift and
move blocks of up to 30 tons (27 t). With the
shift away from derricks has come a shift in the
direction of excavation. Diesel-powered loaders
allow workers to quarry across a horizontal
face instead of excavating the steep vertical face
typical of quarries past. Unk DaRos likens
this new approach to strip-mining.

New Finnish-made equipment now enables
the Castellucci Granite Company to cut 30,000
cubic feet (900 m³) a month. With hydraulic drills
and much-improved explosives, it is possible
now for 10 workers to extract more stone in a

Oswald Worcester (?)
worked the torch and drill
for years in the quarry
business. The pile of old
tires in the background
was used to cushion the
landing for a block of
granite.

187

A gang saw slices a large block of
granite into slabs in the first phase of
fabrication. The vertical blades of the
saw can be adjusted to slice slabs of
different widths. Here the blades are
spaced about 2 inches (5.1 cm) apart.

month than 200 workers were able to cut in any
three years between 1886 and 1910.

The cutting process has also become faster
and more productive. In Providence, the blocks
of stone are sliced like a loaf of bread every 2 to 6
inches (5.1 to 15.2 cm) with a machine called a
"gang saw." The gang saw works by running a

number of steel cables across the block.
Water hoses convey steel shot or, more recently,
crushed steel into a hopper that distributes the
shot under the cables. It is the shot running under
the cables that actually does the cutting. The gang
saw cuts several slabs simultaneously.

These new methods make extraction and
dressing cheaper, reducing the disparity in
cost between Stony Creek granite and any
concrete-glass-steel combination for building.
Nevertheless, quarry owners can only speculate
as to whether the market for granite will
enjoy another surge of popularity like that of
the late 1800s.

Flesh and bone have applied wood, steel,
steam, and jet flame to the enterprise of cleaving
stone from the earth. Given the vast reserves of
Stony Creek granite still in the ground, one
wonders what new technologies will evolve in
the future. Will there be ultrasonic devices for
finding proclivities, lasers for extraction and
cutting, and antigravity devices for loading and
moving the stone? And if there are, will crushed
ankles, burned hands, and other damages to flesh
and bone be a thing of the past? One can hope
that quarry workers will continue to be the
colorful and gritty characters they have always
been—nearly as tough as the stone they harvest.

—RD

AFTERWORD

Indian Summer once again descends on the village of Stony Creek. A century and a half after the granite quarries began full-blown operation, the folks of the village line Thimble Islands Road to revisit the past.

Outside the fire station, two oxen of alarming proportions stand ready to perform their age-old duty. Yoked together and rigged to a white oak sledge, they start their short journey downstreet, transporting a piece of the Stony Creek pink granite that will soon be part of a permanent sculpture installation outside the Willoughby Wallace Memorial Library. This will be the final gift of the Stony Creek Granite Quarry Workers Celebration, a lasting tribute to the quarry workers and their families. After two years of dedicated work, involving dozens of volunteers and a broad range of events and output, a new chapter in the rich history of this place and its times is complete. Or perhaps it is just beginning . . .

OUR THANKS

The Stony Creek Granite Quarry Workers Celebration began as a simple idea. It developed into a multifaceted project that involved the entire extended Stony Creek community. Such was the scope of the project—including the creation of enduring tributes to those whose lives were intertwined with the quarries—that it could only be accomplished through the financial support of individuals and granting institutions. While the fundraising campaign was local and low-key, the response to it was remarkable. Members of the local community gave generously, some with large donations, some with small. Some friends helped by participating in the silent auction of vintage-photograph prints. Others, listed below, gave outright gifts. Some contributors are family and friends of those who worked the quarries. Others simply have an interest in preserving the past and honoring those who preceded us. One and all financial contributors played a vital part in making the Celebration and its outcome a success.

E.C. Adams Middle School National Junior Honor Society
The Altermatt Family
Nina & Greg Ames
John & Marilyn Anderson
David Y. Bailey
In memory of Charles H. & Fannie Page Baker
Paul & Edith Baron
Bob & Jan Beer
Penelope I. Bellamy & Mark Simon
Pauline Bennett
Dana & Lucia Blanchard
Larry Bodkin
Branford Car Wash & Express Lube
Branford Community Foundation
Mavis B. Brittelli
Kenneth P. Brown
Frederick F. Bruening
Dan Bullard & Holly Hopkins
Cameron Construction
Liza Carroll

Dora Lappen Carter in memory of Capt. Dwight H. Carter
Cinda Cash & Bill Walsh
Jane & Leo Cirino
The Connecticut Commission on the Arts
The Connecticut Light & Power Company
Chester W. Cooke
Catherine & John Crawford
The Grandchildren of Richard & Harriet Demato
Mrs. William F. Dow, Jr.
In memory of Benjamin B. duPont
John & Dallas Edwards
Jan Walzer-Etzel & David Etzel
Stan & Debbie Fisher
Paul F. Forman & Barbara Marks
Betty & Wes Foster
Friends of the Willoughby Wallace Memorial Library
Barry Fritz

The Geballe Family
Elizabeth E. Grandel
In memory of Rosario Grandel
Rossi Grandel
The Greenfeld Family
In recognition of three generations of Greenvall quarry workers
Herb & Janice Gruendel
Fran & Donna Guyott
Ron & Gail Halvorsen
Don Hayden, Jr.
Caroline & Kit Henningsen
John Herzan & Lauren Brown
Dana & Warren Hopper
Margaret Ikeda & William Harley
Mr. & Mrs. George C. Izenour
David & Amy Jaffe
In memory of John J. Jakacki
Richard & Katherine Kahan
H. Morgan Keyes & Eunice Keyes Medlyn
Gretchen & Charlie Kingsley

John & Janice Kirby
Tad G. Kumatz
Alan & Linda Landis
Dorothy Leachman
Mr. Kendall & The Rev. Betsey Lewis
Ann Orr Logan
Walter Lowell
Shirley Martin & Bill Allen
Dr. & Mrs. Bruce L. McClennan
Thomas & Patricia McGlashan
Robert & Faith McKenzie
Linda & Jeffrey Meyer
Joan & Jack Moench
Dorothy & Charles Monast
John C. & Marcia H. Murphy
Mr. & Mrs. James S. Nelson

Priscilla Waters Norton
John Opie
Mr. & Mrs. Robert Patton
Thomas & Nancy Patton
Richard & Stephanie Peck
Frank & Marilyn Penna
Kathryn M. Platt
Phil & Eileen Rachelson
Harry & Doris Reimels
Mr. & Mrs. Neal E. Robison
Joanne Scharf
Barbara & Albert Sheppard
Nina N. Smith
The Squaw Brook Co.
In memory of Joseph H. Stamler
Joan & Tom Steitz

Michael & Louise Stocker
Stony Creek Association
Stony Creek Bottle Gas
Emily B. Sweeney & Lee Sweeney
Nancy C. Thompson
Mrs. Elizabeth V. Tishler
Liz & Bill Tower
Garry & Jane Trudeau
The Vlock Family
John Wayland
Jane & Johnathan Weld
Representative Patricia M. Widlitz
Law Offices of Martha Anne Wieler
Carl H. Wies & Margot B. Hardenbergh
Bob Williams & Janny Lehman
Beverly & Dr. Marvin Zimmerman

ACKNOWLEDGMENTS

Our thanks would not be complete without acknowledging those who gave of their time, talents, meeting space, and professional services. Truly, the Celebration and its outcome would have been impossible without them.

Stony Creek Granite Quarry Workers Celebration committee

co-chairs
Judith Robison
Marvin Zimmerman

Jay Ague
Joel Baldwin
Carl Balestracci
Lucia B. Blanchard
Peter Brainerd
Anthony "Unk" DaRos
Kathleen DaRos
Deborah DeFord
Ron DeFord
Paul F. Forman
Betty Foster
Dorothy Greenfeld
Peter D. Hall
John Herzan
Holly Hopkins
Wayne Jacobson
John Kirby
Dorothy Leachman
Barbara Marks
Patricia McGlashan
Jen Payne
Neal Robison
Jonathan Waters
Penny Weinstein
Robert Wilber
Joy Wulke
Beverly Zimmerman

Others who volunteered time, talent, or resources

Glen Arbonies
Rick Atkinson
Florence Banca
John Barnes
Mark Barnes
Theresa DaRos Barnes
Carolyn Lazzari Benni
James Blackstone Memorial Library
Jane Bouley
The Branford Community Foundation
Kenneth Castellucci
Stephen Castellucci
Rosemary Cinquanta
Charles "Tuddy" Collins
Connecticut Commission on the Arts, Art Partnerships for Stronger Communities
Connecticut Historical Commission
Darlene D'Agostino
Albina and Anthony (Tony) DaRos Sr.
Ben DeNardi
Mario DeNardi
Susan Donovan
Peter (Buddy) Dougherty
Mary Dow
Nick Fischer
Friends of the Willoughby Wallace Memorial Library
Jake Greenvall
K&G Graphics
Guilford Free Library

Milton Hubley
Morgan Keyes
Matt Levine
John Loeb
Jeff Marks
Michael and Deborah Marsden
Ron McDermott
Eunice Medlyn
Jay Medlyn
John Murphy
Richard Murphy
Peter Neill
John Opie
Oxen
Mabel and Leonard Page
Projects for a New Millennium
Robert Reynolds
Melvin (Scotty) Robertson
Barbara Sadick
The Sandworms
John W. Shannahan
Stony Creek Association
Jack Swanberg
Thimble Island Shellfish
Sandra Vlock
Willoughby Wallace Memorial Library

REFERENCES

Allen, Donald G. *Barre Granite Heritage with Guide to the Cemeteries.* Barre, VT: Friends of Alrich Public Library, 1997.

Amadon, Elizabeth. *South Station Headhouse National Register of Historic Places Form.* Massachusetts Historical Commission, Boston, MA, and National Park Service, Washington, D.C.: October 31, 1974.

Andrist, Ralph K. and eds. *The American Heritage History of the Confident Years.* New York, NY: American Heritage Publishing Co., 1969.

Baldwin, Rev. Elijah C. *The Home World.* New Haven, CT: Rev. E.C. Baldwin, 1884.

Baldwin, Rev. Elijah C. "Annals of Branford," New Haven *Journal and Courier,* 4 parts, July/August 1879, in John B. Kirby Jr., Stony Creek in 1880, 1979.

Baxter, Linda Trowbridge. *The Newcomers: A Study of Immigrants to Guilford, Connecticut, 1850–1930.* Dexter, MI: Thomson-Shore, Inc., 1985.

Bell, M. *The Face of Connecticut: People, Geology, and the Land: Hartford, Connecticut, Geological and Natural History Survey,* 1985.

Belle, John, and Maxinne R. Leighton. *Grand Central, Gateway to a Million Lives.* New York, NY: W.W. Norton & Company, Inc., 2000.

Berio, Owen. "The Stone of Stony Creek," in Peter Neill, ed., *Stony Creek Miscellanie.* North Haven, CT: John Henry, Stony Creek Fire Company 5, 1975.

Bingham, Harold J. *History of Connecticut,* Vol. 1 & 2, New York, NY: Lewis Historical Publishing Co., 1962.

Boland, Charles Michael. *They All Discovered America.* New York, NY: Doubleday, 1961.

Bouley, Jane Peterson. Research Files. Branford, CT.

Bowen, Ezra, ed. *This Fabulous Century 1900–1910.* Vol 1. New York, NY: Time-Life, 1969.

Bowen, Ezra, ed. *This Fabulous Century 1870 Prelude 1900.* New York, NY: Time-Life, 1970.

Brayley, Arthur W. *History of the Granite Industry in New England.* 2 vols. Boston, MA: National Association of the Granite Industries of the United States, 1913.

Cable, Mary and editors. *American Manners and Morals.* New York, NY: American Heritage Publishing Co., 1969.

Carroll, Liza. *Stony Creek Granite.* Unpublished manuscript. Branford, CT: 1987.

Carroll, Liza, "A Brief History of Stony Creek Quarries," in *Branford: A Commemorative Album, 1644–1994.* 350th Commemoration Album Committee, 1994.

Carroll, Liza. *Mr. Wallace and His Library.* Unpublished manuscript. Branford, CT: Undated.

Carruth, Gorton. *The Encyclopedia of American Facts and Dates.* 9th ed., New York, NY: HarperCollins, 1993.

Chandler, Alfred D. *The Visible Hand: The Managerial Revolution in American Business.* Cambridge, MA: Harvard University Press, 1977.

Clark, Rod, *Carved in Stone: A History of the Barre Granite Industry.* Barre, VT: Rock of Ages Corp., 1989.

Clouette, Bruce. *Elm Street Historic District National Register of Historic Places Form.* Connecticut Historical Commission, Hartford, CT, and National Park Service, Washington, D.C.: October 28, 1983.

Clouette, Bruce. *Bulkeley Bridge National Register of Historic Places Form.* Connecticut Historical Commission, Hartford, CT, and National Park Service, Washington, D.C.: March 1, 1993.

Commemorative Biographical Record of New Haven County, "Hon. William J. Clark," reprint. New Haven, CT: 1902.

Condit, Carl W. *American Building: Materials and Techniques from the Beginning of the Colonial Settlements to the Present. Second Edition.* Chicago, IL: University of Chicago Press, 1982.

Conkling, Philip W. *Islands in Time: A Natural History of the Islands of the Gulf of Maine.* Rockland, ME: Island Institute, 1999.

Dalziel, I.W.D. "Pacific margins of Laurentia and East Antarctica-Australia as a conjugate rift pair: Evidence and implications for an Eocambrian supercontinent." Geology, v. 19, p. 598–601, 1991.

Dwight, Timothy. *Travels in New England and New York.* 4 vols. New Haven, CT: S. Converse, Printer, 1822.

Elliot, S.H. *The Attractions of New Haven County.* New York, NY: Tibbals, 1869.

Erkkila, Barbara. *Hammers on Stone: The History of Cape Ann Granite.* Woolrich, ME: TBW Books, 1980.

Evans, Harold. *The American Century.* New York, NY: Alfred A. Knopf, 1998.

Ferguson, Robert B. "The Story of Battle Monument." Reprint of article from the United States Military Academy, West Point, New York, NY: Undated.

Fitchen, John. *Building Construction Before Mechanization.* Cambridge, MA: MIT Press, 1988.

Gabbaccia, Donna R. "Immigration in the Guilded Age and Progressive Era," University of North Carolina at Charlotte: SHGAPE Bibliographical Essay, www2.h-net.msu.edu, 2000

Gibbs, James. *Old Harbor Historic District National Register of Historic Places Form.* Rhode Island Historical Preservation Commission, Providence, RI, and National Park Service, Washington, D.C.: March, 1974.

Grindle, Roger L. *Tombstones and Paving Blocks: The History of the Maine Granite Industry.* Rockland, ME: Courier-Gazette, Inc., 1977.

Hall, Peter Dobkin. *The Organization of American Culture, 1700–1900: Private Institutions, Elites, and the Origins of American Nationality.* New York, NY: New York University Press, 1982.

Hall, Peter Dobkin. "Organization as Artifact: A Study of Technical Innovation and Management Reform, 1893–1906." In James Gilbert, et al. (eds.), *The Mythmaking Frame of Mind: Social Imagination and American Culture,* pp. 178–208. Belmont, CA: Wadsworth Publishing Company, 1993.

Hartford Evening Post, Souvenir Issue. Hartford, CT, 1908.

Hayes, David F. "The Role of the Finnish Immigrant in the History of Lanesville, Massachusetts, 1870–1957," doctoral thesis. Cambridge, MA: Harvard, 1958.

Helander, Joel. *Oxpasture to Summer Colony: The Story of Sachem's Head in Guilford, Connecticut.* Guilford, CT: privately printed, 1976.

Helander, Joel. *Beattie's Quarry.* Unpublished manuscript. Guilford, CT, 1987.

Herzan, John, John B. Kirby, Jr., and Wayne Jacobson, *The Thimble Islands.* Church of Christ Congregational, Stony Creek, CT. New York, NY: Euro-American Textile, 1999.

Hill, Everett. *A Modern History of New Haven and East New Haven County.* New York, NY: S. J. Clark, 1918.

Holbrook, Stewart H. *Dreamers of the American Dream.* New York, NY: Doubleday, 1957.

In Memorium, William Judson Clark, New Haven, CT: Tuttle, Morehouse & Taylor, 1910.

Jacobson, Wayne E. *Stony Creek Mapanscrap Book.* Church of Christ Congregational, Stony Creek, CT. North Haven, CT: William J. Mack, 1982.

Jacobson, Wayne E. and Anna Symonds. *One Hundred: A History of the Church of Christ Congregational, Stony Creek, Connecticut, 1877–1977.* Church of Christ Congregational, Stony Creek, CT. Includes "Vedder Letters 1863–1879," 1978.

Jennings, Peter and Todd Brewster. *The Century.* New York, NY: Doubleday, 1998.

Keppie, J.D., Dostal, J., Murphy, J.B., and Nance, R.D. "Terrane transfer between eastern Laurentia and western Gondwana in the early Paleozoic: Constraints on global reconstructions," in: Nance, R.D., and Thompson, M.D. (eds.). *Avalonian and Related Peri-Gondwanan Terranes of the Circum-North Atlantic.* Geological Society of America Special Paper 304, p. 369–380. 1996.

Kirby, John B., Jr. compiled & edited. *Stony Creek in 1880.* Includes Rev. Elijah C. Baldwin, "Branford Annals," (history of Stony Creek), New Haven *Journal and Courier,* 4 articles, July/August 1879; Rupert Simons, "Elijah C. Baldwin," excerpts, *A History of the First Church and Society of Branford, Connecticut,*

1644–1919, New Haven, CT, 1919; "The United States Census of 1880—The Village of Stony Creek"; "A Rock Bottom Farm," *New Haven Register,* May 24, 1880; "At Stony Creek," *New Haven Evening Register,* July 17, 1880; "At the Seaside," New Haven *Daily Palladium,* July 22, 1880; "At Stony Creek," *New Haven Evening Register,* August 21, 1880, "Branford," *New Haven Evening Register,* October 7, 1880; 1979.

Kirby, John B., Jr. *Stony Creek Directory, 1900.* Unpublished manuscript. Branford, CT: 1988.

Kirby, John B., Jr. compiled, *Discord in Stony Creek, 1892.* "Stony Creek Enterprise," *New Haven Evening Register,* Aug. 4, 1892; 1992.

Kirby, John B., Jr. compiled. *Stony Creek in 1890, New Haven Register:* "The Thimble Islands," July 24, 1890; "Blown About by the Storm," August 27, 1890; "Capt. Kidd's Treasures," September 4, 1890; 1997.

Kirby, John B., Jr. "List of Substantial Branford and Guilford Granite Quarries," 2000.

Knoll, Mark A., ed. *Eerdman's Handbook to Christianity in America.* Grand Rapids, MI: Eerdman's, 1983.

Landmarks Preservation Commission. *Brooklyn Bridge Landmark Site Report.* New York, NY: August 24, 1967.

Landmarks Preservation Commission. *Grand Central Terminal Landmark Site Report.* New York, NY: August 2, 1967.

Landmarks Preservation Commission. *Statue of Liberty National Monument Landmark Site Report.* New York, NY: September 14, 1976.

Leighton, Eleanor S. *An Historical Study of the Stony Creek Quarries and Their Economic Effect on the Community.* Unpublished manuscript. Branford, CT: 1965.

Losure, Mary and Dan Olson. "Finland Was a Poor Country." NPR News, Minnesota Public Radio, http://news.npr.org, June 6, 1997.

McKenzie, Gertrude Farnham. *A Brief History of Stony Creek.* Women's Auxiliary, Church of Christ Congregational, Stony Creek, CT. New Haven, CT: Van Dyck Co., 1933.

McKenzie, Lee. "The Temperance Movement and Prohibition in the US," Prohibition Party, www.prohibition.org, 2000

McLane, Charles B., and Carol E. McLane, *Islands of the Mid-Maine Coast. Penobscot Bay. Revised Edition.* Gardiner, ME: Tilbury House Publishers, 1997.

McLellan, E.L., and Stockman, S. "Age and structural relations of granites, Stony Creek area, Connecticut: State Geological and Natural History Survey of Connecticut." *Guidebook 6,* p. 61–114, 1985.

Merrill, Frederick J.M. "Quarrying." *Encyclopedia Britannica, Eleventh Edition,* Vol. XXII, pp. 712–713, New York, NY: The Encyclopedia Britannica Company, 1911.

Miller, James W., Priscilla W. Dundon, Jacqueline Reavey, and H. Philip Dudley. *As We Were on the Valley Shore: An Informal Pictorial History of Sixteen Connecticut Towns.* Guilford, CT: Shoreline Times Company, 1976.

Neill, Peter, ed. *Stony Creek Miscellanie.* Stony Creek Fire Company 5, North Haven, CT: John Henry. Includes Owen Berio, "The Stone of Stony Creek"; John Brainerd, "Chronology of Fire"; Liza Carroll, "Notes for an Unwritten History"; and Gertrude McKenzie, "A Brief History of Stony Creek," 1975.

Nevins, Allan & Henry Steele Commager. *A Short History of the United States.* 5th ed. New York, NY: Alfred A. Knopf, 1966.

Northam, Francis Buell. "Stony Crik," in *Favorite Recipes of Stony Creek,* Philonians: Church of Christ Congregational, Stony Creek, CT, 1951.

Paton, Todd, ed. *The Rock of Ages Story.* Barre, VT: Rock of Ages Corp., 1992.

Pitts, Carolyn. *Grand Central Terminal National Historic Landmark Form.* National Park Service, Washington, D.C.: August 11, 1976.

Prann, Perry. "Branford Experiments with Prohibition," in *It Happened in Branford.* Unpublished manuscript. Branford, CT.

Proctor, Redfield. "American Quarrying." In Chauncey M. DePew (ed.), *One Hundred Years of American Commerce,* pp. 188–191. New York, NY: D.O. Haynes & Company, 1899.

Ransom, David F. "Connecticut's Monumental Epoch: A Survey of Civil War Memorials," *The Connecticut Historical Society Bulletin,* Volume 58, Numbers 1–4, 1993.

Ransom, David F. "Connecticut's Monumental Epoch: A Survey of Civil War Memorials." *The Connecticut Historical Society Bulletin,* Volume 59, Numbers 1–4, 1994.

Rockey, J.L. ed. *History of New Haven County.* 2 vols. Includes a history of Stony Creek, CT. New York, NY: W. W. Preston, 1892.

Rodgers, J. *Bedrock Geological Map of Connecticut: Connecticut Geological and Natural History Survey,* Department of Environmental Protection, scale 1:125,000. 1985.

Save Outdoor Sculpture Survey. Connecticut Historical Commission, Hartford, Connecticut, and National Institute for the Conservation of Cultural Property, Washington, D.C.: 1994.

Shore Line Times. Branford, CT: September 22, 1899, and October 13, 1899.

Simons, J. Rupert. *A History of the First Church and Society of Branford, Connecticut, 1644–1919.* New Haven, CT: Tuttle, Morehouse & Taylor, 1919.

Skinner, B.J., and S.C. Porter. *The Dynamic Earth* (4th ed.). New York, NY: John Wiley and Sons, 2000.

Smith, Page. *The Shaping of America.* Vol. 3, New York, NY: McGraw Hill, 1980.

State of Connecticut. *Dedication of the Equestrian Statue of Major-General John Sedgwick Erected on the Battlefield of Gettysburg by the State of Connecticut June 19, 1913.* Hartford, CT: 1913.

Sweet's Indexed Catalogue of Building Construction. New York, NY: Architectural Record Company, 1906.

Taylor, Frederick W., and Sanford E. Thompson. *Concrete Costs: Tables and Recommendations.* New York, NY: J. Wiley & Sons, 1912.

The New Haven Register. New Haven, CT: June 2, 1963.

The New York Times. New York, NY: May 5, 1879, and September 15, 1979.

Turner, Gregg M., & Melancthon W. Jacobus. *Connecticut Railroads: An Illustrated History.* Hartford, CT: Connecticut Historical Society, 1986.

Twohill, Frank B. *Ecology of the Stony Creek Quarry Preserve,* 1982.

Uhl, Charles. *Fulton Building Historic Preservation Certification Application, Part 1—Evaluation of Significance.* Bureau of Historic Preservation, Pennsylvania Historical and Museum Commission, Harrisburg, Pennsylvania: November 1, 1998.

Weisberger, Bernard A. *Reaching for Empire, 1890–1901.* Vol. 8. New York, NY: Time, 1964.

Weisberger, Bernard A. *The Age of Steel and Steam, 1877–1890.* Vol. 7. New York, NY: Time, 1964.

Wetherold, Houghton. "The Architectural History of the Newberry Library." *The Newberry Library Bulletin.* Volume VI, No. 1. November 1962.

Wintsch, R.P., Kunk, M.J., Sutter, J.F., Aleinikoff, J.N., and Boyd, J.L. "Thermochronologic evidence for Alleghanian assembly of 'thermotectonic' terranes, south central New England," McHone, N.W. (ed.), *Guidebook for Fieldtrips in Eastern Connecticut and the Hartford Basin, Northeast Section,* Geological Society of America: 30th Annual Meeting, p. A-1–A-26, 1995.

Withey, Henry F. and Elsie Rathburn Withey. *Biographical Dictionary of American Architects (Deceased).* Los Angeles, CA: Hennessey & Ingalls, Inc., 1970.

Wyckoff, Joseph W. "Monumental Design and Decoration: Some Stock Designs that Ought to be Retired."

Monumental News 27(5) (May 1915), 342–343.
"Simplicity the Keynote in Monumental Design: The Trend of Modern Design away from Ornamentation of Ancient Memorial Art." *Monument and Cemetery Review* (September 1915), 7–9.

ARTICLES

"Census of Stony Creek 1880," in John B. Kirby Jr., *Stony Creek in 1880*. 1979.

"Cornwall is an exceedingly complex subject," www.cornwall-online.co.uk.

"Crusades," "Early WCTS," "Frances Willard," Women's Christian Temperance Union, www.wctu.org, 2000.

"Emigrants and Emigration—The Cornish American Connection," www.chycor.co.uk.

"Origins of the Foreign Born Population, 1860," www.albany.edu, 2000.

"Prohibition," "Socialism," "Temperance," *Funk and Wagnall's New Encyclopedia*. New York, NY: Funk & Wagnalls, 1973.

"Prohibition," "Temperance," *Encyclopaedia Britannica*. 15th ed. London: Britannica, 1974.

"Prohibition," "Temperance," *Encyclopaedia Britannica*. London: William Benton, 1965.

"Stony Creek/Thimble Island Historical District, Branford, CT." Registration form. National Register of Historic Places, Connecticut Historical Commission, 1988.

"Stony Creek's Plea," Stony Creek, CT: Church of Christ, fundraising brochure, 1901.

"Stony Criker." Newsletter for World War II military. Vol. 1, Nos. 1 & 2, 1943–44.

"The Stone Bridge at Hartford, Conn." *Engineering Record* 50: December 31, 1904.

"Vedder Letters, 1863–1879, compiled by Anna Symonds, in Wayne Jacobson, *One Hundred*, Church of Christ Congregational, Stony Creek, CT. North Haven, CT: John Henry, 1978.

ILLUSTRATION CREDITS

© Peter Aaron/Esto: 155 (2)
Joel Baldwin: VIII, 48 (10), 150 (2)
Courtesy of the Boston Public Library, Print Department:
    154 (left)
Jane Bouley: 148 (left)
Phil Carloni: 157
Kenneth Castellucci (Photography by Etta DeBiasio):
    128–129, 138
Church of Christ Congregational, Stony Creek: 147
Earl Colter Studio: 148 (right)
Courtesy of Connecticut Department of Environmental
    Protection: 15
Guilford Free Library: 35, 159
From The Guilford Keeping Society Library Collection: 36
Hartford Collection, Hartford Public Library: 153 (top),
    161 (2)
Photograph by Joel E. Helander (1968): 42
John Herzan: 160, 164
Courtesy of John B. Kirby: 39 (from New Haven, CT City
    Directory 1900)
Map image courtesy of Maptech, Inc.: 44, 45
Michael Marsden: IX, 10
© Peter Mauss/Esto: 156
Ron McDermott: 149
The National Archives Still Picture Branch: 158
The Newberry Library: 152 (2)
Tools assembled by Leonard Page: 48
Robert Reynolds: 12, 13 (3)
J.W. Swanberg Collection: 28 (left)
Charles H. Uhl: 153 (bottom)

Many of the images used in this book came from the archives of the Willoughby Wallace Memorial Library in Stony Creek, Connecticut. These archives would not exist were it not for the generosity of those individuals and families who have allowed their photographs to be included in the Library's collection. We have endeavored to attribute photographs from the archives to their original sources; where this has not been possible, we have credited the Willoughby Wallace Memorial Library as their source.

Theresa Barnes: 6, 47, 60, 65 (2), 130, 132 (2), 133, 134 (3),
    135, 136 (3), 154 (right), 187 (2)
Peter Brainerd: II–III, 74 (2), 80, 86 (bottom right),
    88 (top right)
Christy Photo: 52 (2), 69, 78 (bottom), 139
Mary M. DaRos: 16, 128
Photography by Etta DeBiasio Studio: 188
C.H. Dibble 35 Winters: 110
Rose Russell Edwards: 1, 56, 70–71, 75, 76 (top), 78 (top),
    82 (top), 88 (bottom), 89 (top right), 94, 104,
    163 (bottom), 184
Photo by Foster, Brooklyn, NY: 85
Jake Greenvall: 95, 123, 137 (top)
John B. Kirby: 27 (left)
Lazzari family: 50, 77, 81 (left), 88 (top left), 90, 98, 99,
    109, 111, 115, 126–127, 131, 137 (bottom), 171, 173,
    179 (right)
Ron McDermott: 64, 72–73, 79 (bottom)
Medlyn family: VI, 24, 97, 106–107, 142
Rogers Photo: 92
C.A. Russell, Photographer: 21, 27 (right), 28 (right), 87,
    89 (bottom left), 182
Photo by John B. Russell: 83 (top)
Willoughby Wallace Memorial Library: 1, 2–3, 18, 59, 62,
    63, 66, 67, 76 (bottom), 79 (top), 81 (right), 82 (bottom),
    83 (bottom), 84, 86 (top), 86 (bottom left), 89 (top left),
    89 (middle), 89 (bottom right), 108, 124–125, 140, 163
    (top), 166, 172, 179 (left) 186

INDEX

The image on the endpapers is of polished Stony Creek granite shown at two times actual size

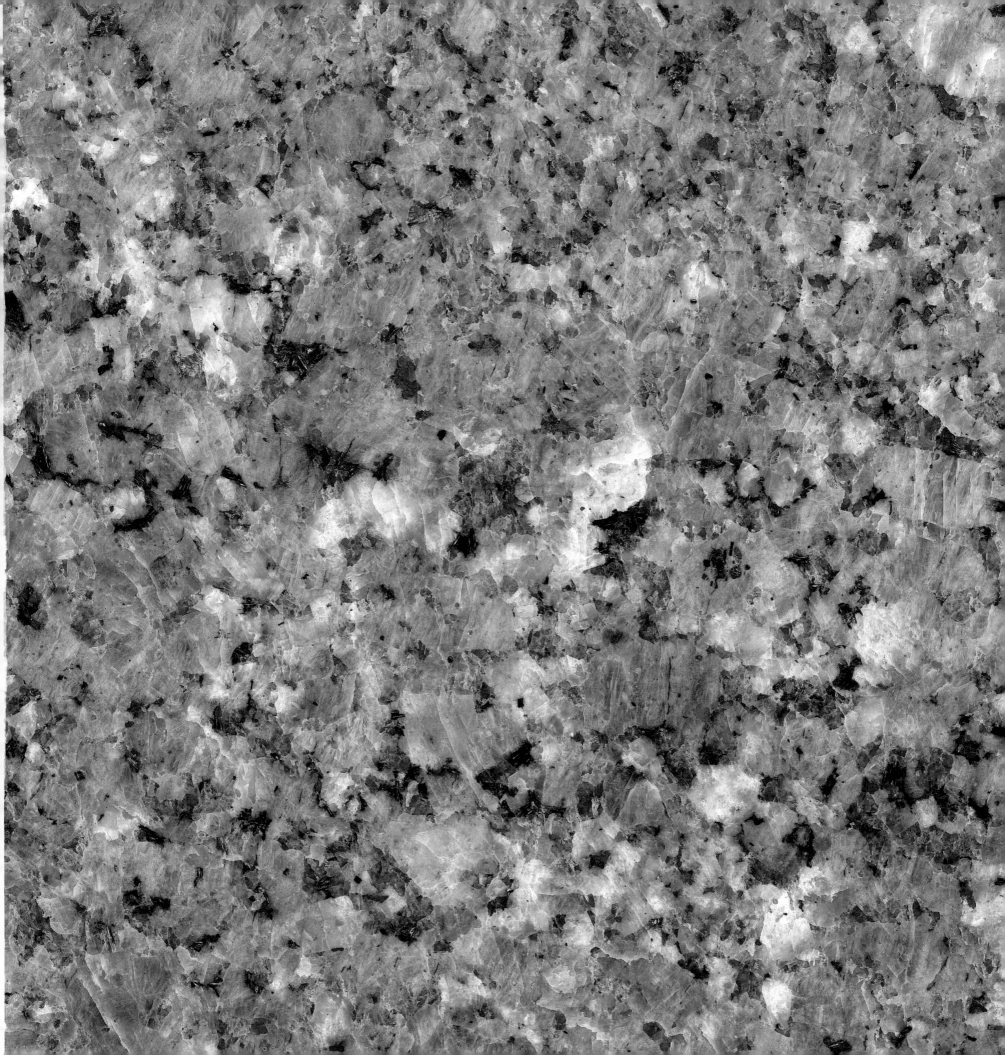

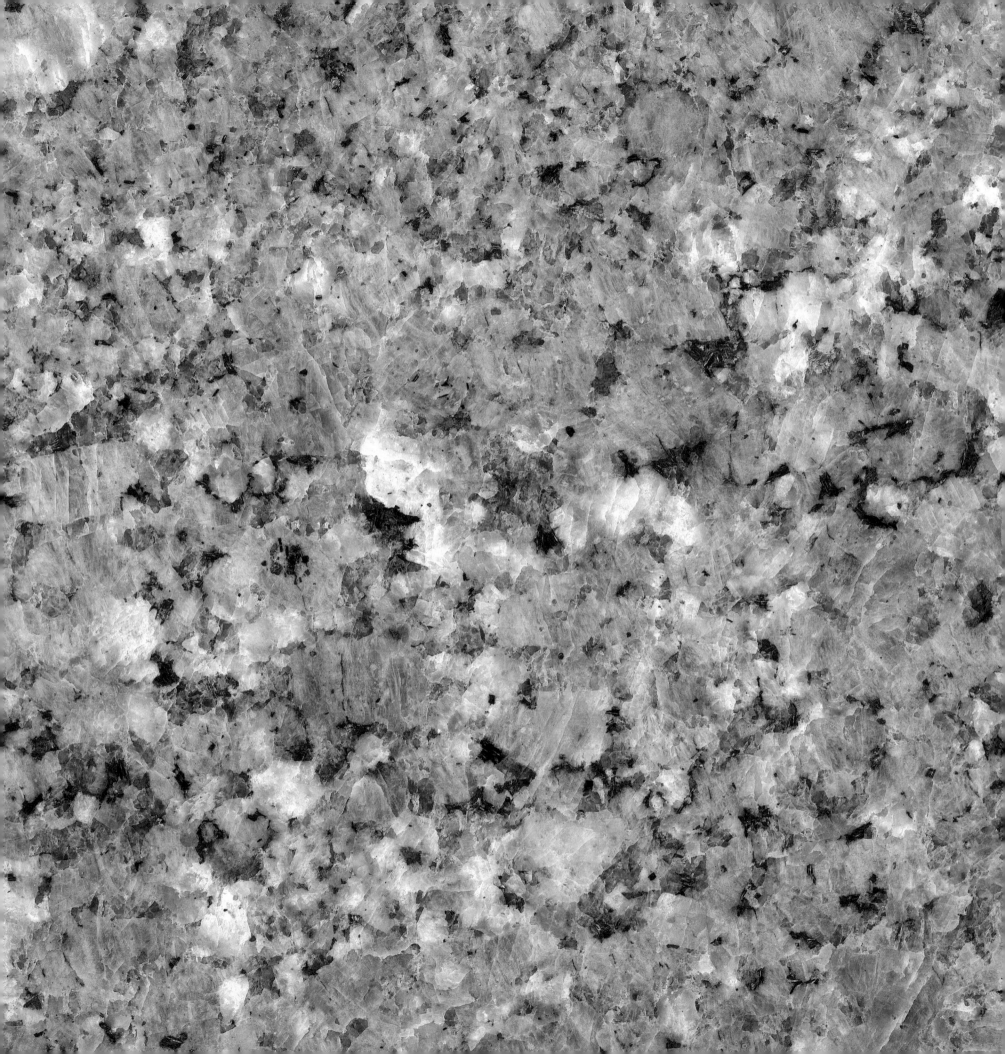